MULE ▮▮ DEER
C O U N T R Y

Text by
Valerius Geist

Photography by
Michael H. Francis

To Greg & Nina,
This could be your
backyard! Enjoy the
photography.
Michael H. Francis 1992

NorthWord
PRESS, INC

Box 1360, Minocqua, WI 54548

Library of Congress Cataloging-in-Publication Data

Geist, Valerius.
    Mule deer country / by Valerius Geist; photography by Michael
Francis.
        p.   cm.
    ISBN 1-55971-076-4 : $ 39.00
    1. Mule deer.   I. Francis, Michael H.   II. Title.
    QL737.U55G43   1990
    599.73′57--dc20
                                                                90-43851
                                                                    CIP

Designed by Origins Design, Inc.

NorthWord Press, Inc.
Box 1360
Minocqua, WI 54548

For a Free Catalog describing NorthWord's line of nature books and gifts,
call 1-800-336-5666.

ISBN 1-55971-076-4

Printed in Singapore

Michael H. Francis, born in Maine, has spent the past twenty-one years as a resident of Montana. He is a graduate of Montana State University. Previous to becoming a full-time wildlife photographer, he worked seasonally in Yellowstone National Park for 14 seasons.

Mike's photography has been internationally recognized for its beautiful and informative nature imagery. His work has been published by the National Geographic Society, The Nature Conservancy, The Audubon Society, and *Field & Stream*, *Outdoor Life*, and *Natural History* magazines, among others. He is currently rounding out a portfolio of photographs illustrating the natural history of North American elk, in another author-photographer collaborative effort with Dr. Valerius Geist, for a book to be published by NorthWord Press in 1991.

Mike lives in Billings, Montana, with his wife Victoria and their daughter Elizabeth.

Before beginning the monumental but enjoyable task of compiling a photographic chronicle of the life of the mule deer, I possessed in my files, like many other wildlife photographers, numerous photographs of mule deer bucks in autumn. More than ten years worth, in fact. Yet these photos really didn't relate much about this magnificent animal. I wanted to know and photograph the more-intimate details of the lives of mule deer. Thus the odyssey which found me traveling the Rocky Mountain West for almost two years, following, observing and photographing the day-to-day activities of this fascinating species.

During and long before that odyssey, many people unselfishly extended me their help and guidance. Without it, this book would never have been possible.

My mother and father, Derline and John, raised me to believe in myself, to know that no goal was too lofty for me to achieve if I once set my sights on it. They also taught me to love and respect the outdoors and wild animals. Some of my fondest early memories are of duck hunting with Dad. He had me convinced that my cap-gun "six shooter" was more than just a child's toy, taught me that hunting was a privilege, and to revere ducks and any other quarry we hunted. My mother allowed my inquisitive mind great latitude by sharing our home with the baby field mice, lizards, turtles and other wild animals I brought home.

Without the moral and financial support of my wife, Victoria, this project would have been impossible. She often stayed home alone with our daughter, Elizabeth, for long periods of time, yet she was always willing to give me the encouragement I needed to keep focused on my goal.

Special thanks also to my good friend Ron Shade, who spent thousands of hours in the field with me these past ten years. We've enjoyed photogrpahing not only mule deer but any other wildlife his sharp eyes happened to locate.

My special gratitude to those friends who were helpful and generous and, after showing up at their homes after a week in the field, provided a warm bed and a hot shower, including the Russell family: Charlie, John, Sandi and Valerie Haig-Brown. Their hospitality, good conversation and valuable tips were greatly appreciated.

Others who didn't mind taking in a ragged wildlife photographer include Shane Moore, Ken Houseman, John Heiser, Karen Semerau, Paul Bechtold, Jeff Olson, and Mary and Jim McCaleb. Thanks for always making me feel welcome in your homes, especially during those long, cold, stormy winter evenings.

The mule deer have very special friends in Phyllis Hazen and Roger Sebesta, and Dr. Richard Mackie of Montana State University, who was regularly available to provide me with valuable information on the species.

I wish especially to thank Dr. Valerius Geist. I only wish I had read his informative text for this book ten years ago; it would have saved me considerable time and effort in the field. I am grateful that someone who has devoted so much time and energy to the study of mule deer would be so willing to share such a wealth of information. I hope our joint efforts in producing this book provide the reader a privileged, inside view of the marvelous world of mule deer country.

Valerius Geist is a professor of environmental sciences on the Faculty of Environmental Design at the University of Calgary at Alberta, Canada. He obtained a Ph.D. in zoology in 1966, specializing in ethology (the study of animal behavior), from the University of British Columbia, Vancouver, where he worked with Dr. Ian McTaggert-Cowan, whose work on the taxonomy of mule deer (1936) remains definitive to this day.

After a year of post-doctoral study in Germany with Konrad Lorenz, Dr. Geist took a position at the University of Calgary where he became a founding member of the Faculty of Environmental Design as its first Program Director for Environmental Sciences. He published one technical (1971) and one popular book (1975) on his work with mountain sheep and edited, with Fritz Walther in 1974, a two-volume conference proceedings on the behavior of ungulates. He has also been a consultant or co-editor for numerous other books, including some published by the National Geographic Society. Currently he is completing a monograph on the deer family.

His scientific work has been honored by the American Association for the Advancement of Science, The Wildlife Society, the Foundation for North American Wild Sheep and other organizations.

In addition to his published technical works, Geist has had more than 70 popular articles published in outdoor and natural history magazines. He is the wildlife columnist for *Western Sportsman* magazine and serves on the editorial boards of numerous scholarly journals.

Dr. Geist's research has focused mainly on the biology and evolution of large Ice Age mammals, but also on policy matters in wildlife conservation. The basis of his research for this book stems from field and experimental studies of mule and white-tailed deer that were done primarily since 1969.

Conservation is a major focus of Val Geist's work. He acts as an expert witness in investigations pertaining to breaches of conservation legislation in Canada and the United States, in environmental impact assessments and public hearings. He serves on committees with the International Union for the Conservation of Nature, the Conseil International de la Chasse, Wildlife Habitat Canada, The World Wildlife Fund, Canadian Society of Zoologists, Alberta Society of Professional Biologists, The Canadian Committee for the International Biological Programme, the Frankfort Zoological Society and others.

Val met his wife, Renate, when both studied biology at the University of British Columbia. She teaches German and is a translator with several published volumes to her credit. The Geists have three grown children, a daughter and two sons, and are now grandparents. Renate is an avid gardener and hiker, Val a wilderness buff, hunter and fisherman.

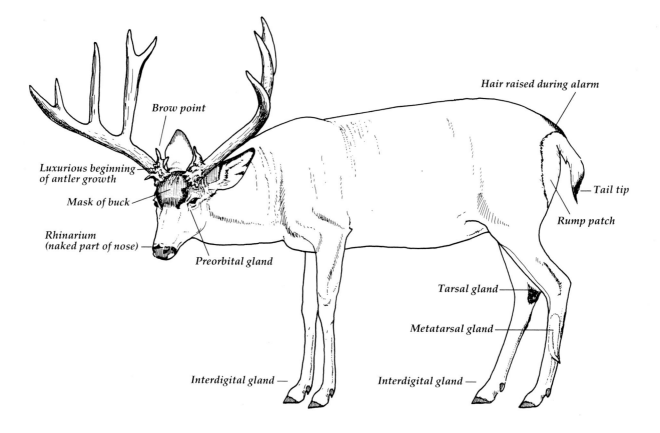

Hair raised during alarm

Brow point

Tail tip

Luxurious beginning of antler growth

Rump patch

Mask of buck

Rhinarium (naked part of nose)

Preorbital gland

Tarsal gland

Metatarsal gland

Interdigital gland

Interdigital gland

RHINARIUM: Refers to the black, naked, moist portion between the nostrils.

PREORBITAL GLAND: This gland is located just before the eye and can be opened wide when the deer is excited. It is not used for scent marking.

FACIAL MASK: This is the very dark coloration above the eyes and the very light color of the rostrum or nose. It indicates that the individual is a buck.

INTERDIGITAL GLANDS: Glands located between the two hooves on each leg. Externally one can see, just above the hooves, fat-stained hair, caused by the secretion of this gland.

METATARSAL GLAND: This is a long gland located on the outside of the lower hind leg (metatarsus). It is a long, horny ridge surrounded by elongated hair. In mule deer this gland is 4-6 inches long, a size diagnostic or unique to mule deer. The gland functions in alarm responses.

TARSAL GLAND: These are the tarsal "brushes" on the inside of the hocks (hind legs). The gland is composed of specialized hair that absorb lactones from the urine, which give this gland its distinct, pungent smell. The deer urinate on this gland and rub the two brushes together, priming it with scent. Males have a characteristic distribution of lactones; females and yearling males have another. That is, immature males smell like females. The gland-hairs are flared when the deer is excited. The deer's identity appears to reside in the smell of its tarsal glands.

RUMP PATCH: The mule deer has a permanent rump patch that is always visible. It can be enlarged somewhat by a flaring of the hair, which happens in alarmed deer, when the tail-hair is also flared.

TAIL TIP: The tail tip appears to function as an attention catcher. The tail tip is exposed during dominance displays and hidden by subordinate deer.

BLACK HAIR AT TAIL ROOT: This hair is flared during alarm (when the tail is depressed).

CHAPTER 1

IN THE BEGINNING

*Sunset on the prairie. Mule deer will often
hide in small draws all day and come out to
feed as the sun goes down. When the sun rises,
they will once again retire from sight.*

*The rugged badlands of the West
are home to many mule deer.*

He is North America's deer of scenic mountains and foothills, of forsaken, rugged badlands, of windswept, delicate prairies and harsh, desolate brushlands. Usually larger, more rugged and bulkier that the white-tailed deer of eastern forests, his large mule-like ears give rise to his common name, although he shares little other resemblance to his domestic namesake. He is the mule deer.

The mule deer (*Odocoileus hemionus*) is a flashy newcomer on the North American scene, a descendant of the successful old-timer, the white-tailed deer. And, because of unusual circumstances in its evolution, we say that the mule deer descended not once, but twice, from the whitetail, as will be explained. We suspect, too, that the white-tailed deer may ultimately be responsible for the mule deer's demise as a species. The paradox of two separate genetic origins is but one remarkable and peculiar aspect of the mule deer's story and of how this deer came to be. No less intriguing is the idea that the whitetail, the mule deer's progenitor, may cause its genetic oblivion. In any discussion of the life of the mule deer, then, it is essential to look first at the history of its ancestor, the white-tailed deer.

The white-tailed deer (*Odocoileus virginianus*) is the oldest of all the deer species in the western hemisphere, and that by a very large margin. It first appears in the fossil record in the southern part of North America some four million years ago. This indicates that it arose from temperate zone deer when the high Arctic was still a land of forests and lakes, not of tundra and polar deserts, and continental glaciers were still to come. Those early whitetails, according to the famed paleontologist Bjorn Kurteen, at least in their hard parts that were

*A mule deer doe, left, sharing an area
with whitetails. Mitochondrial DNA studies
suggest that mule deer are descendants
of whitetail mothers and blacktail fathers.
When hybridization between the two species
occurs today, it is usually observed in forested
areas where their ranges overlap.*

preserved through fossilization, appear to be identical to today's representatives of the species. The white-tailed deer, then, is something of a living fossil. Still, the whitetail is an outrageous success because it has not changed much – if at all – over millions of years. Not changing, not evolving while being able to take great environmental changes in stride, is the hallmark of biological success.

Originally the whitetail was a species of warm temperate landscapes. Its geographical origin lies somewhere to the north of southern North America, but we cannot pinpoint exactly where. It first appeared when cooling climatic conditions terminated the then existing subtropical fauna of southern North America some four to six million years ago, creating the favorable temperate environment that suited the biology of the whitetail. Verification of this, however, is not directly possible. Almost all of northern North America was subsequently ground over by enormous continental glaciers. Consequently, almost all the potential fossil-bearing deposits between two and 65 million years of age that could provide substantiating evidence of the species' origins have been scraped away, erased by glacial action.

Undisturbed preglacial deposits of four to six million years of age are found beyond the southern margins of the glaciers, namely in the continental United States, and again at the northern edge of glaciation in arctic Canada. It is in these deposits that paleontologists have found the scant evidence that does exist of our earliest whitetails. However, no other deer of any description are found in any of these deposits that predate the fossil appearance of whitetails and their relatives. Conditions for the preservation and fossilization of animals in these deposits in arctic Canada, though, were not favorable.

FIGURE-TIME SERIES (BP = before present, M = million years)

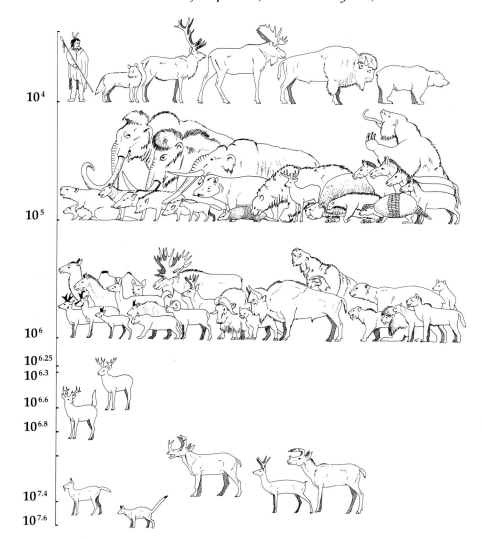

10^4 **(10,000 BP)** *A wave of Siberian immigrants, man included, enter North America on the heels of the decline of North America's species-rich megafauna. A new, raw, poorly adapted fauna assembles, made up of Siberian newcomers and old, opportunistic North American species (white-tailed deer, black-tailed deer, pronghorn, peccaries, black bear, coyote). The mule deer arises as a hybrid species.*

$10^5 - 10^6$ **(10,000 – 1 M BP)** *A species-rich specialist fauna evolves on in North America, formed from South American immigrants (ground sloths, glyptodonts, armadillos), Siberian immigrants (mastodons, elephants, bovids, cervids, large cats, bears) and old indigenous mammals (horses, camels, pronghorns). It reaches at least 65 species of large herbivores and carnivores before extinction at the end of the last Ice Age. Several major Ice Ages come and go.*

$10^{6.25}$ **(1.8 M BP)** *The major Ice Ages begin periodically covering northern North America with a huge ice sheath. Some Siberian species enter as indigenous North American late-Tertiary species die out.*

$10^{6.3}$ **(2.0 M BP) Odocoileus** *appears on the West Coast. This might be the beginning of the black-tailed deer. Primitive moose, a New World deer, appear in Europe. Deer enter South America.*

$10^{6.8}$ **(6.0 M BP)** *Lush deciduous forests, much like those once grow in in the east of North America, cover the high Arctic. This is the most likely home of New World deer. Acid conditions favor the fossilization of wood, but not bone.*

$10^{7.4}$ **(25.0 M BP)** *A tropical grassland fauna rich in camels, horses, but also in uniquely North American ruminants, evolves on the continent. Some of the most grotesque ruminants ever to evolve appear in America, as exemplified by horned camels (Protocerata) and merycodontids, ancestral to the pronghorns.*

$10^{7.6}$ **(40.0 M BP)** *Primitive ruminants enter North America from Eurasia. Small in size and well armed, they probably defended territories and hid much of the time in thick undergrowth.*

Some six million years ago the high arctic was clad in forests not too different from those that exist today in Vermont and New York. It is reasonable to suspect, but is speculation nonetheless, that these preglacial northern forests were the home of the ancestors of our present-day deer. These early representatives of the genus *Odocoileus*, to which today's mule deer, black-tailed deer and white-tailed deer of the western hemisphere belong, are believed to have evolved in the northern part of the New World, and to have have traveled to the south of North America with deteriorating climates. As climates cooled with the onset of continental glaciation, these ancestral deer spread south of the future glacial margins. A million years after the New World deer made their appearance in North America, they also appear for the first time in the fossil record of Europe.

The fossil record, then, indicates that the temperate climate species, the white-tailed and the black-tailed deer, emerged first, beyond the ice margins, and the cold-adapted species, such as caribou, appeared much later on this continent, after the beginning of continental glaciations and during a time when the ephemeral land bridge between Siberia and Alaska was in existence as a result of lowered sea levels. In the interim, whitetails, with their ability to cope with warm climates, eventually ranged as far south as South America. The later-evolving cold-adapted species, however, such as moose, roe deer or caribou, never penetrated into subtropical climates.

The white-tailed deer spread slowly after its appearance. It took over a million years before it found its way to the west coast of North America, where it evolved into the black-tailed deer. In old deposits, identification of the species of these two deer is not certain because

the bones of black-tailed and white-tailed deer are so very similar.

The slow spread of the early whitetail's range is not necessarily surprising. Our deer are highly specialized "opportunists" or "weed species" that lived then in densely packed communities of specialized herbivores and diverse carnivores. Deer, apparently, were not common. The white- and black-tailed deer existed by virtue of high reproductive rates, rapid local dispersal, rapid skimming of whatever highly nutritious forage was available, and being tested by many different predators.

The opportunistic way of life is a specialization in its own right, the very opposite to narrow specialization on certain foods. The greater the competition from the narrow food specialists about them, the greater the selection pressures these early deer experienced for extreme opportunism and adaptability to change. It came in handy repeatedly to the whitetail, for it survived several great faunal changes on this continent, including a great wave of extinction that occurred 7,000 to 14,000 years ago and peaked about 10,000 years ago. Only after the extinction of the many specialized herbivores and carnivores did whitetails become abundant in the post-glacial fossil record.

That great change swept away North America's large, unique association of giant mammalian herbivores and carnivores. At least 50 of some 65 species vanished and were replaced with rather poorly adapted Siberian immigrants, including the cold-adapted deer species – elk, moose and caribou – as well as grizzly bear, the timber wolf, and man. Also remaining were the primitive opportunists that were part of the old North American fauna, foremost among them the white- and black-tailed deer, and also the pronghorn antelope, the

To the left are the New World deer (A-N) whose origin resides most likely in the late Tertiary of North America and eastern Siberia. To the right are a selection of Old World deer (O-U) whose origin resides in mid-Tertiary Southeast Asia. Both subfamilies of deer evolved during the Ice Ages, the bizarre-antlered giants in northern latitudes. However, the New World deer invaded South America early in the Ice Ages and in a very short time evolved a great variety of deer, from giants (now extinct) to dwarfs, such as the Pudu, which may weigh as little as 13 pounds when grown.

A. This represents a small, tropical, tusked deer from the tropics of the Old World. It is the probable ancestor of all deer. The long, sharp canine teeth of males indicate that it defended a territory. All primitive deer were "saltors" that ran by jumping.

B. *Hydropotes inermis*, the Water Deer of China and Korea is a cold-adapted version of primitive tusked deer. Usually placed into its own subfamily, it stands close to the New World deer.

C. *Pudu mephistophiles*, the Northern Pudu, living in the northern Andes, is at 11-13 pounds live weight the world's smallest deer.

D. *Mazama gouzoubria*, the Gray Brocket is a widely distributed, small, territorial South American deer. This is a secondarily primitive deer that is closely related to white-tailed deer.

E. *Ozotoceros bezoarticus*, the Pampas deer, a small, gregarious deer renowned for its pungent odor, is now close to extinction.

F. *Hippocamelus bisculus*, the Huemal, is a short-legged mountain deer, goat-like in build. Like all South American deer which evolved without a wolf-like predator, this deer is highly endangered by dogs – as well as by humans.

G. *Odocoileus virginianus*, the white-tailed deer, is not only the oldest known deer species, but has also the largest latitudinal distribution: It is found from just south of the Arctic Circle in Canada, to 18° south of the Equator in South America.

H. *Odocoileus hemionus*, the mule deer of North America.

I. *Blastocerus bezoarticus*, the Marsh Deer, is the largest South American deer. An ecological specialist from the Tropics, it is in danger of extinction.

J. *Capreolus capreolus*, the roe deer. This genus is widely distributed in the temperate and cold parts of Eurasia. It has evolved a surprisingly large number of similarities to the Pronghorn, despite having virtually no relation to the latter and preferring dense cover to open plains.

L. *Libralces gallicus*, the first moose to be found in the fossil record. The size of an elk, it had the build of a speedy runner and was thus a plains dweller. It was, however, a foliage feeder as its teeth are identical in structure to those of the current moose.

M. *Alces alces*, the extant moose of Eurasia and North America. It's a "trotter" that sheds predators by making them jump continually over low obstacles it can clear without body lift.

N. *Cervalces*, the North American Stag Moose. It became extinct after the Ice Ages. As large as an Alaskan moose, it had, besides large, three-lobed antlers, longer legs and larger hooves. Its nose was unlike that of the modern moose.

O. The most primitive of the Old World deer are the muntjacs which arose in the mid-Tertiary. Here is *Muntiacus reevesi* from China, the smallest, most generalized and widely distributed.

P. *Rucervus eldi*, the Elds deer from tropical Southeast Asia is a highly specialized swamp deer. It is of a primitive body plan as are all tropical Old World deer.

Q. *Rusa unicolor*, the Sambar, an elk-sized coarse-grass eater widely distributed in Southern Asia. It is a tropical giant of primitive build.

R. *Dama dama*, the Mediterranean Fallow deer is a small-bodied descendent of fallow deer as they first appeared in the early Ice Ages. It changed little. It belongs to the giant-deer branch which was most numerous in the early Pleistocene.

S. *Cervus nippon*, the Sika deer appeared before the Ice Ages. It is adapted to cool, wet winters. This is the ancestral group to the red deer-wapiti radiation of the Ice Ages.

T. *Megaloceros gigantheus*, the Irish Elk, was the last of the many giant deer to survive. It was highly adapted to speedy, enduring running and thus to open, fairly warm, and very productive landscapes. It was as large as a big moose, but carried twice the antler mass. It showed some parallels with the caribou in adaptation.

U. *Cervus canadensis*, the Wapiti, is the largest and most highly evolved of the red deer. The largest wapiti during the last glaciation rivaled Irish Elk in size. This is a deer well along in adaptations to running, though it falls short of Irish Elk and caribou. The advanced Wapiti of North America and Siberia originated in Ice Age Beringia and are virtually indistinguishable.

black bear and the ubiquitous coyote. These animals, relieved of predation and competition, multiplied and spread!

For the greater part of their history, though, prior to extinction of North America's large herbivores and carnivores, the white-tailed deer in the east and the black-tailed deer in the west were severely hemmed in. The trees, shrubs and grasses about them were continually under assault by the large herbivores whose destructive foraging patterns resulted in a mosaic of fluctuating plant communities. Where such large herbivores were common, they removed much of the mature vegetation and broke up burnable plant communities into small patches. The small patches of vegetation were not conducive to destruction by wild fires set by lightning, except on a localized basis.

With the extinction of the "megaherbivores," however, plant communities in the whitetail's range eventually changed to expansive, more uniform associations susceptible to fire. Eventually, in much of that range, repeated wildfires cleaned out mature vegetation and encouraged sprouting and recolonization by plants, creating an abundant food supply for deer and other comparatively small herbivores.

The huge, hot wildfires that swept inferno-like over the prairies and forests of North America, and which are so vividly described by the terrorized early settlers, are thus an artefact of megafaunal extinction. And regardless of how man views the destructiveness of such fires, the infernos are a boon for deer. After large wildfires, huge areas of excellent deer habitat appear. Our deer, with their high reproductive and dispersal rates, exploit this to the hilt. While whitetails and blacktails were rare when the many large herbivores and carnivores controlled

*The mule deer can swivel its large ears
to detect danger from any direction and at
relatively long distances. The resemblance of the
deer's ears to those of a mule gave rise to the
blacktail's common name of mule deer.*

the land, they became very abundant after the extinction of the megafauna.

In the absence of the large carnivores and the expansion of large areas of favorable habitat, whitetails and blacktails not only became abundant, they also expanded their range. The white-tailed deer expanded north and west, and the black-tailed deer expanded east – and then the two met. And that meeting is crucial. It created the western mule deer.

Not too long ago, researchers using new investigative tools for determining hereditary codes discovered that that meeting of blacktails and whitetails provided the genetic origin of the mule deer. The research was based on studies of DNA of the three forms of deer.

Within our cells we carry not only a genetic code in nucleic acids (DNA) within the nucleus, but also in the nucleic acids of the "power houses" of the cytoplasm, the mitochondria. The nucleic acids in the mitochondria are called mitochondrial DNA. The significance of the mitochondrial DNA is that it is inherited through the female line. That is, your cells are powered by mitochondria you inherited from your mother, and her mother, and her mother and so on. One can thus trace an individual's maternal origins through the mitochondrial DNA.

When researchers compared the mitochondrial DNA of mule, white-tailed and black-tailed deer, they were quite surprised. The mule deer, the most highly evolved of the black-tailed deer, had mitochondrial DNA almost identical to that of the white-tailed deer. The black-tailed deer and the white-tailed deer, however, were far apart. If the mule deer runs on white-tailed deer mitochondria, then it means that all mule deer are descendants of white-tailed deer mothers and black-tailed deer fathers.

Since there is so little difference between the mitochondrial DNA of mule and white-tailed deer, it means that the mule deer originated rather recently. And that suggests that black-tailed deer expanding east over the Rockies, and white-tailed deer expanding west, met and hybridized, with black-tailed bucks displacing white-tailed bucks from reproductively receptive whitetail does. Consequently, the white-tailed deer participated in the making of the mule deer twice, once in the distant past, when it gave rise to the western black-tailed deer, and once again in the recent past when it hybridized with blacktails.

Furthermore, the mitochondrial DNA studies indicated that there were several independent origins of mule deer out of white-tailed deer mothers and black-tailed deer fathers. It happened in several localities along the mountain front. And, curiously, not only is the mitochondrial DNA of mule deer similar to that of white-tailed deer, it is somewhat more similar to that of white-tailed deer in the south and east than to that of white-tailed deer in the west, which mule deer today commonly meet and live beside. This suggests that an effective barrier to hybridization evolved between mule and white-tailed deer in the west, a conclusion entirely supported by the behavior of the two species. There are today two behavioral barriers to hybridization in natural populations of these two deer. As we shall see, when hybridization does occur today it is the result of human interference.

The real miracle is that a hybrid species could succeed at all. As we shall also see later, hybrids between mule deer and whitetails have insurmountable problems. Each species has a unique, finely tuned survival system. Hybridization destroys these specific survival systems, and the hybrid is fit for neither way of life. Hybrids between species can often thrive

Some of the most scenic mountain areas in
North America are habitat of mule deer.

under human care and protection, but when exposed to predators, bad weather and competition, they do not thrive.

A hybrid species can arise only under exceptional circumstances – when there is a virtual absence of predators and competitors. That condition was almost certainly produced 7,000 to 14,000 years ago by North Americas's period of megafaunal extinction. And so it seems, given the facts at hand, that among the Siberian mammals now native to this continent, and the indigenous old-timers that survived the Great Extinction, the mule deer stands out as the only newly evolved species. It is thus the most recent of deer to arise as a distinct, new form.

CHAPTER 2

SURVIVING PREDATION

Under ordinary circumstances, most coyote-killed deer are crippled, diseased or young animals. In times of deep crusted snow, however, even large, healthy animals are vulnerable as they lose mobility and sink into the snow. The lighter coyote, able to stay on top of the snow crust, can then easily run down its prey.

*Mule deer are sometimes referred to as
"jumping deer" because of the stiff-legged
bounding gait they employ with all four feet
off the ground. This "stotting" allows them
to escape predators that they might not
otherwise be able to outrun and enables
them to jump over obstacles that a
pursuing animal must go around.*

In a deer's life, security is paramount, and escape behavior is an essential part of that security. Spook a mule deer and you will see it bound off with high, stiff-legged jumps. We call this escape behavior "stotting." It is an odd way for a deer to run.

It is puzzling, at first examination, why a mule deer should stott, because it can gallop very fast, nearly as fast as the white-tailed deer. In social games, when chasing a companion or running from a pesky fly, the mule deer runs off at a gallop. When disturbed by a predator or humans, however, it stotts off. Obviously, there must be something terribly advantageous about stotting for the mule deer to slow down his escape, rather than speed it up, in the face of danger.

Spooked in a deep ravine, a mule deer may bound like a jackrabbit, straight up the slope and over the top – a remarkable feat. Spook a whitetail in the same area and it sprints off, but down the slope. When the mule deer reaches the top it may stop to look back at you, something you don't expect from a white-tailed deer. As in so many other instances, though, the two deer species act in opposite ways.

So, what is advantageous about stotting? It actually slows down the deer in an emergency, since galloping is faster, although not much faster than stotting. Stotting is also very costly in energy. Bodily lift requires about 13 times the energy expired in equivalent horizontal movement. Also, why is stotting innate to mule deer but nonexistent in whitetails? Hybrids between mule and white-tailed deer cannot stott, but only bound. Even $7/8$ mule deer and $1/8$ white-tailed deer hybrids bound, but do not stott. Clearly, stotting must be an escape tactic under close genetic control, and, consequently, fully exposed to natural selection.

*Mule deer are known to collectively "mob"
and rout predators such as coyotes. This
small group of deer has spotted a coyote
sleeping in a prairie dog town. The coyote,
awakened, rises and begins to turn away
from the deer, then runs away as first one
and then all the deer chase after him.*

Years ago the great American naturalist Ernest Thompson Seton chased mule deer with greyhounds and horse through the western badlands. He noted that while his greyhounds easily gained on mule deer in open terrain with even footing, the mule deer got the better of his dogs as soon as they hit broken terrain. With ease and grace the mule deer sailed up the steep badland hills, leaving the dogs in a shambles. And that is one clue to the advantages of stotting and why it is the mule deer's primary anti-predator strategy: It places obstacles in the path of pursuing predators. These obstacles may be tall bushes or windfalls; deep and wide gorges; and even gravity, in the form of steep slopes and highly uneven footing in sharply eroded terrain. It is little wonder, then, that mule deer prefer habitat containing such obstacles, for there they can exercise effectively their innate locomotory capacities.

Stotting not only gains height to clear obstacles and provide a better view of the runway ahead, it can be used to economically ascend near-vertical walls, to space the deer's tracks far apart, making tracking difficult, and to allow an instant and unpredictable change of direction. A stotting mule deer can suddenly depart at right angles to his line of travel, and even jump backward. Moreover, stotting allows mule deer to "mob" predators. Unlike whitetails, mule deer may quickly charge and strike coyotes: They may even unite with other mule deer for this act and give a small predator a merry chase.

In all this the mule deer is diametrically opposed to the white-tailed deer. While mule deer are quite ready to attack small predators, whitetails choose to depart. The whitetail maximizes distance between itself and a predator by running at high speed, deliberately avoiding obstacles. Consequently, the whitetail makes and sticks to runways – the mule does

not. Even wounded whitetails will, on snow, run along some sort of a trail, including the tracks left by a hunter. The whitetail uses gravity to accelerate to high speed and notoriously winds up in valley bottoms and in or near water. The mule deer ascends. Whitetails may break from cover to sprint across obstacle-free terrain. In essence, they maximize distance between themselves and a predator. This apparently allows the whitetail's scent to evaporate, confusing the predator and slowing it down. This is a conclusion reached by Professor Larry Marchinton and his colleagues from experiments of radio-collared deer and hounds.

These are only some of the differences in anti-predator strategies between mule and white-tailed deer. Both hide, but respond quite differently to approaching danger. In essence, the white-tailed deer stays hidden and allows the danger to pass. If the danger is too close, it bursts from its hiding spot with a great crash that startles and surprises. Then it accelerates to high speed along some trail. The mule deer does things differently. It scans the surroundings with its incredibly keen ears, and, when it detects approaching danger, it may not remain hidden if it is in rather dense, extensive cover. Rather, having analyzed the nature of the danger, it rises and quietly leaves the valley at a walk. This may occur when a hunter, for instance, is still a quarter of a mile or more away. In fact, quietly leaving the area where trouble is imminent is the most common response of the mule deer. It is a very effective way for it to save itself from dangerous situations. I am aware of one mule deer buck in one of my study areas who had a badly deformed leg. It could not run, but it survived at least two years with that handicap in an area with very heavy coyote predation. Upon detecting something amiss, he would hobble at once behind a bush, lie down and scan for potential danger, then get up and

Bucks tend to hide more often than does,
sometimes sneaking off to avoid danger
and other times hiding in very little cover
while waiting for the danger to pass.

leave. He ignored my presence. Like many mule deer I have observed over extended periods, he had seen me many times and was accustomed to my not posing a threat to him. Consequently, he acted normally in my presence and allowed me to watch his actions.

In the prairie, where cover is scarce, or in small, isolated clumps of shrubbery in the foothills, I have seen mule deer hide tenaciously in cover and allow a person to approach within a few yards. It appears that bucks tend to hide more than does and also tend to have a system of departure all their own. When a hunter approaches, for instance, does may stott off as a group in high bounds, but bucks will often continue resting and then walk calmly away after the hunter has gone.

Also, when severely disturbed by humans, bucks and does exhibit different longer-term behavior changes. My colleagues and I have explored this experimentally on radio-collared mule deer. Does responded to harassment with more hiding, disrupted daily rhythm, and finally with a loss in reproduction, but remained loyal to their home ranges despite our continued disturbances. The harassed bucks left their home ranges at once for unknown distant quarters. They went so far that we could not find them despite the radios they carried. Occasionally they returned, as evidenced from radio signals, only to leave again. These short reappearances may have served as scouting trips to determine whether we researchers were still active on their home range.

These are not the only instances when a buck and doe act quite differently. When attempting to capture mule deer with a net gun operated from a helicopter, it is easy to catch does. When the helicopter swoops behind a doe, she is likely to stott away from the aircraft in a

straight line, allowing accurate aiming of the net gun and rapid capture. Not so with bucks. They dodge back under the helicopter, and it takes many tries and misses with the net before a buck is captured.

It should be no surprise that buck and doe mule deer act differently when disturbed. The buck is much larger than the doe. That makes him more capable of fighting, but a poorer runner. Muscle power does not increase proportionately with mass; therefore, the buck has relatively less power to move himself, despite larger muscles. In fall, a rather large portion of a buck's mass is nothing but fat that he needs for the rutting season. Also, to be a fighting machine, he has a lot of muscle mass on his shoulders and neck that, like his fat, contributes little to stotting or running. He can't be as speedy, as agile or as enduring as the doe, and being the last in a herd of deer fleeing from predators is an invitation to disaster. So, the mule deer buck has different emphases on security strategies from those of the doe, and one finds a similar sexual bias in white-tailed deer.

When I have followed, a few paces to the rear, some of the tame but free-roaming bucks in my study areas, they showed me again and again how keen of ear, eye, and mind they were. Long before I noticed a distant deer, they were already aware of its presence. Minutes later I would finally hear or see the animal they were approaching. They followed attentively the appearance of a deer as far away as 600 yards. Their eyesight, clearly, is excellent. Only when it came to spotting resting deer was I regularly their superior. They could not make out does or bucks resting quite close to their line of travel, as long as these did not noticeably move. Resting deer allowed both the deer I was following and me to pass closely, but, again, the deer

in the area were accustomed to my presence.

The large ears of the mule deer are like radar detectors swiveling to and fro, catching faint distant noises. A large buck showed me one day how quickly it used its ears to analyze happenings in its surroundings. I had discovered the big buck with a doe in heat. So had a small buck. The old fellow chased off the youngster repeatedly, but to little avail, at least initially. Again and again the youngster crept back, and each time he was chased off. Then, he left for good. The big fellow, apparently thirsty, made some movements, quite hesitantly, towards a lake about 200 paces away. He started to walk toward the shore, then stopped and scanned for the bothersome little buck. Satisfied that nothing moved, he finally walked off to have his drink. When he was about 100 paces away from me and his doe, I stepped forward and accidentally snapped a small stick. Instantly, the big buck spun around and ran back. I raised my hand and equally instantly the buck spun around again and walked off to have his drink. Having seen me wave, he connected the snapping of the stick with me, not with his pesky rival.

It is its combination of keen ears and eyes, its calm disposition and great propensity to learn that, in forested country, makes the mule deer so very much harder to hunt than the white-tailed deer. In open landscapes neither deer is a great challenge to an experienced hunter. In forests, white-tailed deer, for all their secrecy and nocturnal habits, can be induced to show themselves or can be expected to appear along certain trails. Not so mule deer bucks. Their propensity for random roaming, the large size of their home ranges, and the great sensitivity of their ears all ensure that the stalking or even the sitting hunter will experience the greatest difficulty harvesting them.

*Spooked mule deer will usually head straight up
the nearest hillside and only stop upon reaching
the top to look back at the impending danger.
This type of behavior would never be
expected from a whitetail.*

Random roaming. It is difficult to label it any other way. Much of the time, feeding and wandering mule deer act as if they do not know where they will move to next. In tagging along with them I discovered that we both had pretty much the same idea of what constitutes an ecological hotspot for the does. The bucks moved quite predictably along the shortest routes between these hotspots. The moment one would decide to feed, however, that predictability vanished.

It is difficult to investigate "randomness" and I can't claim to have done it effectively. Theoretically, a powerful random component in minute-to-minute movements is a boon to the deer's security. And if a deer does not act predictably, then no predator can clue in on its whereabouts; if the deer does not know where it will feed or rest, neither can a predator.

While conducting my field studies I could not foretell from day to day where the deer would be that I watched the day before. Nevertheless, I usually had no difficulty finding them. Within the very large home ranges of the female clans, the females had certain preferred areas, which I call ecological hotspots. A systematic approach of these was all that was required to make contact with most individuals I had seen the day before. However, that changed when coyotes entered the area and successfully preyed on the fawns.

The response of the deer to these killings was dramatic. First they dispersed and went into hiding. Then they left the area in an organized fashion, in groups, swimming across a large lake to its distant, and possibly more secure, shore. In the initial dispersal most of my study deer left the valley floor and could be found several thousand feet higher, at the edge of timberline of the adjacent mountains. When snow was on the ground I could easily track them

*Coyotes are proficient at driving young deer
onto ice-covered lakes during the winter months.
Once on the slippery ice and unable to gain footing
and affect an escape, the deer become easy prey.*

right to their beds until I stood beside them. They would look at me from below the snowed-over branches of dwarf spruce or through the maze of twigs of dense willow thickets. They were utterly calm and even ruminated while watching me. This docile, tame behavior exhibited by these deer is one of the differences between mule deer and all but a minority of white-tailed deer. I have known only one white-tailed buck that would allow me to accompany him, even lie down beside him where he rested. Once it is habituated to the non-threatening presence of a human, such tolerance is not unusual for a free-living mule deer.

The coyotes and wolves hunting mule deer in my study area in southern Alberta, or in various areas where I spent time following deer, taught me several lessons about mule deer security strategies. These strategies, however, contained fatal flaws, at least to young deer. A fairly certain way for predators to catch young mule deer in late fall was for coyotes to patrol the upper edges of steep ravines leading down to frozen lakes. Here they would spook deer. While the adults bounded away parallel to shore and to safety, some youngsters would bound down onto the lake ice – and become prey to the coyotes. Again and again I found the carcasses of young mule deer on the ice within a hundred yards of shore. After several such killings the deer began to leave the valley.

We know, from several studies, that coyotes are effective predators of young mule deer. Timber wolves are apparently even more effective. In the forests of Jasper National Park, wolves sometimes kill mule deer far in excess of their numbers relative to the number of elk and moose present. Yet the deer survive in Jasper.

And so do they in the northern Rocky Mountains of British Columbia where they

*During the fawning season, both
black and grizzly bears may spend
considerable time hunting for newborn
mule deer. Bears also kill and eat crippled
or sick deer or deer incapacitated by
old age, but more often than not they
appropriate deer killed by coyotes
or mountain lions.*

are also under heavy pressure from wolves. Such were my observations while studying Stone's sheep in this as-yet-roadless wilderness where mule deer live not far from the 60th parallel, close to their northern limit. I was present during the rut, and the tracks of mule deer crisscrossed the valley of the big Ketchika River, but try as I may I could not see these deer. Only once in four weeks of daily field work did I spy a female and her fawn, resting in the sunshine on a tiny clearing on a south-exposed slope. These deer hid very well, and judging from the wolf tracks I encountered they had frequent cause to hide.

It may well be that the abundance of mule deer in recent decades is in part the result of wolf extinction over most of the mule deer's range. Nevertheless, the mule deer can survive wolves as can the white-tailed deer. That is more than one can say of the coastal Sitka deer, the most primitive member of the black-tailed deer species. It is found on Alaskan coastal islands along the panhandle, but not on the mainland where wolves are found. It survives well with the giant brown bear, but experimentally released wolves on islands rapidly decimated this small deer. The inherent deficits in its anti-predator strategies, as well as those of the adjacent Columbian black-tailed deer, remain to be studied.

The mule deer's stotting, successful in open, but broken terrain, and successful against single pursuing predators, is probably not very effective in forests and against pack hunting wolves. Nor does the mule deer appear to be too capable at avoiding mountain lions. We know that once mule deer detect a lion in their vicinity, they leave at once for distant places. Otherwise we remain ill-informed about the deer's security strategies against lions. Are the mule deer's ears capable of discerning this predator's approach? How mule deer handle crisis

Although usually adept at negotiating fences, mule deer occasionally become entangled in the wire strands and suffer a slow, agonizing death.

situations at night, when so many predators are active, we do not know.

What we do know is that mule and white-tailed deer differ diametrically in much of their security behavior, because the primary thrust by one species is to search out obstacles and the other's is to avoid them. This has had deep repercussions on each deer's biology. For instance, in order to evade successfully a pursuing predator, a stotting mule deer must jump aside only when the predator lunges to bite. Only then is the predator guaranteed to miss. If the deer deviates earlier, so can the predator. Consequently, to successfully evade a predator, the mule deer must be not only watchful of his back trail and his flight path, it must, compared to the whitetail, also remain supremely composed. And, compared to whitetails, that is what mule deer appear to be. In addition to being able to escape from sight of a pursuing predator, mule deer also, by their relatively calm behavior, give no clue to weakness.

Calmness may well be the prerequisite to becoming so utterly tame, as unhunted mule deer tend to become. They readily seek out human habitation and become, in some locations, rather unobtrusive residents whose only victims are gardeners struggling to grow exotic shrubs and flowers. In Waterton National Park's townsite, where mule deer and humans have now co-existed for generations, the deer are a part of the town's fixtures. Mule deer love the town! Coyotes and mountain lions do not enter. Delicious fertilized lawns provide the deer essential green-feed in winter as the vortices whirling about houses always create some snow-free areas. And all those steep house walls must create some sense of security in the deer, who rest among the houses. Towns can be ideal places to live, not only for people. 🦌

CHAPTER 3

TODAY'S MULE DEER & HIS RELATIVES

*The mule deer is, despite its
still enormous range, a shrinking
species, a species in trouble.*

Figure 1. Geographic range of (1) Rocky Mountain mule deer, (2) desert mule deer, (2a) Tiburon Island mule deer, (3) California mule deer, (4) Southern mule deer, (4a) Cedros Island mule deer, (5) peninsula mule deer, (6) Columbian black-tailed deer, and (7) Sitka black-tailed deer.

Today, mule deer are found from just south of the Arctic Circle in the Yukon Territory of Canada to central Mexico, and east of the High Sierras and coastal ranges of California, Oregon and British Columbia into the prairie states and provinces. Three subspecies of the mule deer proper are recognized by some specialists, but all three subspecies are very similar in external appearance. They are: the Rocky Mountain mule deer (*Odocoileus hemionus hemionus*), the desert mule deer of Arizona and northern Mexico (*O. h. crooki*) and the burro deer (*O. h. eremicus*) from southwestern Arizona, southeastern California and northwestern Mexico.

There is little doubt that these are distinct ecotypes of mule deer, but there is legitimate doubt that they are actually distinct subspecies. That is, in their appearance, behavior and ecology, we need not doubt that these deer reflect the habitats in which they live. We may doubt, however, that there are genetic differences responsible for all the observed differences.

The eastern boundary of the mule deer is in flux. It has contracted and receded much in the east and central portions of the mule deer's range, and there is no indication that this apparent decline has stopped. The mule deer is, despite its still enormous range, a shrinking species, a species in trouble. It is much the same animal wherever we meet it throughout its range, not a very surprising observation if the animal is as recent an evolutionary form as discussed earlier. But it also shows signs of maladaptation, as do other members of North America's large mammal fauna.

At its northern rim of distribution, for instance, mule deer may be seen with badly frozen, that is, bulbous, deformed ears. Long extremities fare badly during cold snaps in

northern winters, giving credence to an ecological axiom, the so-called Allen's Rule. It states that animal forms in cold climates have relatively shorter appendages (ears, tails, and legs) compared to relatives in warm climates, a reference to cold-climate adaptations and the direct relationship between the surface area of large extremities and their high heat loss. Caribou living in the same northern regions as mule deer show what cold-adapted ears look like: They are short, round and thickly furred. Obviously, the mule deer in the central Yukon do not have ears to match the winter climate.

One would expect great changes in mule deer as one moves from the cold Yukon to the deserts of Arizona and Mexico. However, the differences between Canadian mule deer and Mexican ones are truly modest in external appearance. It may be, though, that appearances deceive. White-tailed deer from northern South America and those from North America are also remarkably alike, but in genetic distance they are further apart than are white-tailed deer from black-tailed deer. By contrast, the white-tailed deer has been a long time in South America, has adapted to local climatic and forage conditions, but has retained the social behavior of its ancestors, as have North American whitetails. One often finds that social behavior changes less than external appearance. Whitetails in Venezuela may breed and bear fawns year around, a classical adaptation to tropical conditions of species that hide their young. (Social ungulates from the tropics, though, which bear highly developed young, tend to bear them all in a very short time span annually.) Whitetails also have regimes of coat shedding adapted to tropical climates, such as retaining the red summer coat for most of the year or growing an incomplete winter coat.

Antler size is an indication of a buck's vigor.
Very large antlers grow only under conditions
of surplus food, and symmetrical antlers only
grow on a buck with a healthy body.

While the mule deer in its southern distribution is called a desert deer, one must not take that designation literally. The "desert" mule deer is very much tied to areas near open water and is largely nocturnal. It does well, though, growing to large size, and mature bucks sport exceptionally large, symmetrical antlers. The latter is an excellent sign, for antlers are a deer's barometer of foraging success and health. Large antlers can grow only under conditions of surplus food, and symmetrical antlers only on a very healthy body. Small, crooked antlers spell trouble. It's the more remarkable then that the desert mule deer's range does not extend farther, but just as the black-tailed deer along the Pacific Coast are found in a restricted range, so the mule deer remains confined to northern Mexico. White-tailed deer are found to the south of this mule deer population, mostly as diminutive specimens.

Maladaptations haunt North America's large mammal fauna. We note, by way of example, that the Sitka blacktails and timber wolves do not co-exist well in Alaska. Of the wolf we know that he is a Siberian newcomer. Of the black-tailed deer we know that it lived on the west coast of California during the period of continental glaciation (Pleistocene) with quite different predators. Other examples of maladaptation include the disrupted synchrony of antler growth and reproduction of elk in California. Female elk in California populations ovulate over an extended period, and the first ones come into heat before the bulls have even shed their antler velvet. Consequently, the bull elk begin to bugle, fight and rut while still in velvet antlers. And, in the southern parts of its range, the desert bighorn sheep is still a "northerner" struggling to adapt to desert conditions. Introduced "real" desert sheep, such as the Barbary sheep from the Sahara, have no such difficulties. Another newcomer on the

*Adult bucks and does differ greatly in their
facial characteristics. The doe's face is almost
a uniform color, but the buck's is marked
by the sharp contrast of the brow patch
to the light-colored rostrum and cheeks.*

continent, another Siberian immigrant, the moose, cannot cope with the parasitic brain worms and ticks of the white-tailed deer, and elk have difficulties with some parasites of mule deer. Excepting man, none of the Siberian immigrant species have penetrated beyond the mountain ranges of northern Mexico to the south, as did white-tailed deer. In short, the signs of maladaptation by mule deer are shared with others, and along with the fact that neither mule deer, nor elk, moose, bison or grizzly bear differ greatly in external appearance across great geographic distances speaks for a young post-extinction fauna in the process of adapting.

In sharp contrast to the struggle of the Siberians with southern latitudes, or the southerners with Arctic winters, reintroduced "old Americans" are doing much better than native wildlife. Donkeys, horses and camels, whose ancestors all originated on this continent, and which have been missing from this continent only a fraction of one ten-thousandth part of one percent of their history, have been a notable success wherever they have become feral. They are successful in deserts, prairie or foothills. They spread and multiply to become serious competitors with wildlife and domestic stock until eradicated. It is as if their genetic make-up still made them fit into North America's biota and climates. These American expatriates even thrive on plants so poisonous that they are hardly touched by today's wildlife or livestock.

On the Pacific Coast, the black-tailed deer, unlike the mule deer in the continent's interior, has differentiated geographically in external appearance. Most like its white-tailed deer ancestor is the Sitka deer (*O. h. sitkensis*) from the Alaska panhandle and the north coast of British Columbia. Seen from the rear, the average buck or doe of this subspecies is surprisingly similar to whitetails, except for the facial mask that characterizes blacktails and mule deer. The

*Depending upon the season, terrain and
other factors, mule deer may be prone
to making long, seasonal migrations.*

late Olaf C. Wallmo, a dedicated life-long student of mule and white-tailed deer, was very taken by the similarities of this little deer to whitetails. It is relatively short-legged, with the smallest metatarsal glands of all blacktails, a tail brown on top and antlers that, save for the absence of a brow tine, are similar to those of whitetails. It runs more like a whitetail than a mule deer. It lives in the coastal rain forests where it makes seasonal movements between the lush subalpine vegetation at timberline in summer and the sea coast in winter. When glaciers covered the interior of California, this little deer may have lived in cool, wet coastal forests similar to those in coastal Alaska today.

South of the range of the Sitka deer stretches the great range of the rather similar Columbian black-tailed deer (*O. h. columbianus*). Members of this subspecies may live in prodigious densities in coastal habitats all the way to southern California; it hybridizes with the mule deer along the crests of the coastal ranges. It varies greatly in body size, depending on the habitat, but in external appearance it can be recognized by its dark tail, the beginning of a rump patch, and the relatively large metatarsal glands. We still do not know its security and social behavior in detail, but what is available is tantalizing. This deer appears to form, unlike others of its genus, bisexual clan territories.

However, what goes on in black-tailed deer society is all too often shielded by nearly impenetrable thickets of leatherleaf, alder, bracken fern, huckleberry and huge windfalls of impassable chaparral on coastal slopes. Still, we know that individual groups of bucks and does of the *columbianus* subspecies unite to defend a commonly held piece of ground against other Columbian black-tailed deer. Even strangers experimentally introduced into large

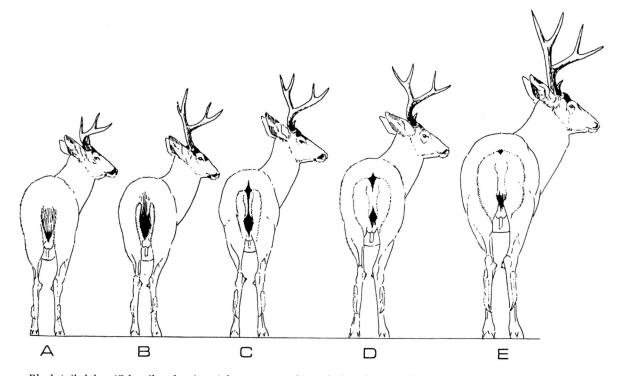

A   B   C   D   E

Black-tailed deer (Odocoileus hemionus) form a geographic and altitudinal gradient in which individuals change in appearance from the most primitive subspecies, (A) the Sitka deer (sitkensis), to the most advanced, (E) the Rocky Mountain mule deer (hemionus). The graduation in external appearance follows ecological changes from wet coastal forest to dry shrub-forest to dry subalpine and desert. In short, the mule deer occupies the climactically extreme habitats of all black-tailed deer. The Sitka deer, found in coastal Alaska, is joined to the south by (B) the Columbian black-tailed deer (columbianus). The Columbian black-trailed deer joins (C) the Californian mule deer (californicus) in southern California. This deer occupies the western slopes of the Sierra Nevada. To the west is found (D) the Inyo deer (inyoensis) who might be a hybrid between Californian and Rocky Mountain mule deer (E). Desert mule deer (crooki and eremicus) are recognized as a different subspecies, but differ little from Rocky Mountain mule deer in external appearance. In southern California and Baja California are found the Southern mule deer (fulginatus) which looks like a very dark Columbian black-tailed deer (peninsulae) and the small, near extinct Cedros Island subspecies (cerrosensis).

enclosures within coastal forests eventually united into territory-defending clans. Much of what one sees these deer do to one another fits with territorial defense by clans. Black-tails check out each other often at the tarsal gland. They form groups whose members get along well, but are hostile to apparent strangers. Small and young clan members pester large ones with attention, as if reinforcing their "belonging." These Columbian black-tailed deer are prone to attack marauding dogs, they run not unlike mule deer, but they stott less. Their legs are noticeably shorter than those of mule deer. However, it is not clear what this difference means.

The Columbian blacktail changes to the southern mule deer (*O. h. fulginatus*) along California's south coast, and as it progresses to higher elevations into the peninsula of Baja, California, it becomes the peninsula mule deer (*O. h. peninsulae*). There is even an island dwarf, the Cedros Island deer (*O. h. cerrosensis*), which lives far off the coast of Mexico. These blacktails along the coasts retain very much the Sitka deer's preference for moisture and cool temperatures; where low elevation deserts, such as those found in Baja, California, block their way, they seek cool uplands in favor of hot lowlands.

At about the latitude of Los Angeles the blacktail turns inland and continues as the California mule deer (*O. h. claifornicus*) on to the western slopes of the Sierra Nevadas. Thus, Columbian blacktails live on the coastal side of the large inland valleys of California while California mule deer live on the continental side.

The California mule deer differs from other blacktails by having a much more mule deer-like tail and rump patch, long metatarsal glands and the tendency to grow a four-pronged mule deer-like set of antlers. On the heights of the Sierras one finds the Injo deer

*The Rocky Mountain mule deer, especially in
areas where it receives little disturbance,
is active during daylight hours and
readily wanders about its range.*

(*O. h. inyoensis*), a subspecies more like Rocky Mountain mule deer than the California mule deer. The Injo deer may well be a hybrid with the Rocky Mountain mule deer; it may also be a more highly evolved California mule deer. An analysis of its mitochondrial DNA might tell.

One thus finds what is technically called a "cline" of black-tailed deer, beginning with the small Sitka deer from wet, cold coastal forests in Alaska and ending with the large mule deer of extreme climates, the high mountains and the hot deserts. The various subspecies differ by progressive differences in antler size and shape, but even more so by progressive differences in rump patch, tail and metatarsal gland size.

In all this movement into various habitats, the black-tailed deer repeated what happened in distantly related Old World deer, as well as sheep and goats: Habitation of regions with increasingly more extreme climates and greater seasonality eventually lead to larger bodies, complex and larger antlers and more ornate coat colors and patterns, especially about the rear quarters.

The Rocky Mountain mule deer is quite ornate with its erectile rump patch and bluish gray or reddish coat that grades into black on the chest. It has a distinct facial mask and large, sharply pointed ears, relatively large, complex antlers (larger than those of the white-tailed deer), and is a more odorous, noisy and gregarious deer than the whitetail. The mule deer may also make long seasonal migrations, is a day-active animal where not disturbed, and wanders about readily in the open where whitetails living in the same localities will venture only after dusk.

It is notable that the mule deer's antlers are larger overall than the whitetail's. In

*A young mule deer must be able to keep up with
its mother. Although small, the fawn must follow
her and be capable of running and jumping
over obstacles in order to avoid predators.
One physiological survival strategy of mule
deer, rapid growth of the fawns, means
that the doe must contribute heavily
from her own body's resources during
gestation and while lactating.*

deer and other ruminants, antler size and ornateness increase with gregariousness and preference for open landscapes. Clearly, the mule deer, compared to the whitetail, fits that description. That, however, also suggests that there is some female choice, or positive reproductive selection, for mates with large antlers.

Very large antlers are associated with high-speed endurance running, which is an anti-predator strategy. It is here mandatory that a young of the year be able to keep pace with its mother. To be able to do that it must be born highly developed, have a relatively large body size, and it must have rich milk to allow it to rapidly outgrow the dangerous juvenile stage, when it is especially susceptible to predation. It means, too, that the mother must be most capable of sparing resources for foetal growth and milk, resources that would otherwise go to her own body's maintenance and growth. If so, then the father's ability to spare resources from growth expresses itself as large antlers, because antlers are universally highly sensitive to forage surpluses.

To the female, large antlers are expected to be attractive, allowing mate selection for superior fathers, a process which, in turn, produces offspring of the best genetic constitution. As expected, one finds that, in deer, relative antler mass in males correlates positively with the relative size of the fawns or calves at birth, with the percentage of dry matter in the female's milk, and with increased antler displays by the males in courtship of females, but not with threats or displays to other males.

We would therefore expect that, on average, mule deer does would bear larger fawns than white-tailed does, that the fawns would spend less time in hiding, that the milk of

*Mule deer bucks display their antlers to does during
courtship, and antler size may be a determining
factor in the doe's selection of which bucks
she will allow to breed with her.*

mule deer does is richer than that of whitetail does, and the mule deer bucks employ their antlers in mating displays, to which the does are attentive. So far, however, there is no data on any of these points to point decisively to their factual existence. However, whatever differences might exist between the two species are not likely to be large (and thus difficult to measure), in part because of the mule deer's youth as a distinct and separate species that evolved from the whitetail.

In Europe, the fallow deer stotts in a somewhat similar manner to the mule deer. This, like high-speed running, is a specialized, energy intensive form of escaping. We note that fallow deer have the highest relative antler mass among Old World deer, that they bear rather large young that soon follow their mothers, that the does have rich milk, and that the males greatly advertise their antlers in courtship and that females choose among bucks on small breeding territories. The fallow deer, however, compared to the mule deer, is a fairly old species that appeared in its current shape in the middle of the Ice Age in Europe.

Do mule deer pay attention to antlers? There is no experimental evidence, as exists for red deer, to answer this question. Mule deer appear to recognize each other individually by antler shape, for, as I have repeatedly noted in snow storms when the antlers of mule deer bucks became covered with snow, the bucks make mistakes in identification until they can smell one another. Large bucks that were so similar in external appearance that I had initial difficulty in distinguishing them also posed problems of identity to other mule deer bucks.

While it is tantalizing to conclude that during courtship a mule deer buck's eye-aversion from the female constitutes a display of his antlers, this "display" behavior lacks all

the ritual one finds in fallow deer. Huge old mule deer bucks that have regressed antlers, long spikes and wavy forks that are but caricatures of their once-large, symmetrical racks, have no difficulty dominating large-antlered bucks and winning breeding does. Dominance roughly parallels antler size, but so does it body size, and the old regressed bucks show only too clearly that antler size as such matters little in dominating rivals or obtaining breeding females. Since the large master bucks remove all rivals from their breeding area prior to breeding, no mule deer female in heat would have another large buck in view for comparison, as would an estrous fallow deer female who has the opportunity to choose among several bucks, all in sight on their small breeding territories. ♦♦

CHAPTER 4

FOODS & FEEDING

*Mule deer fawns are born in the spring soon
after the does have reached their summer range.
The gangly offspring weigh from six to seven pounds
at birth. They give off very little scent and remain
motionless when bedded. These traits and their
camouflage coat help foil predators such as
coyotes, bears, eagles and bobcats.*

*The mule deer's red summer coat appears
after the winter pelage is shed in spring.*

Summer is a glorious time in the Rockies, particularly when the alpine is in bloom. The air is fresh and crisp, the nights cool, the days not too hot. Mosquitos and biting flies may be about, but on dry, windy ridges they offer no great problem. An occasional rain shower or thunderstorm with spectacular clouds and lightning may disturb one's romance with Mother Earth, but the sun breaking through the clouds on green, sparkling meadows, and a full rainbow restores one's faith and spirit. White snowfields trim the high peaks, and distant glaciers may shimmer blue in icy grandeur. The timbered valleys trail off in blue infinity.

Throughout the mountains, nature is renewing itself. White-crowned sparrows sing at timberline. Golden mantled ground squirrels and chipmunks scurry about; picas squeak and display their industry as little hay piles in the rocks. Bighorn ewes, serious, attentive mothers, look up from grazing to the gang of playing lambs – and up to the eagle soaring past. The eagle has already learned, however, that there is little profit in diving at lambs. Their mothers are too attentive and much too ready to strike with their horns. The lambs are large now and beyond easy hunting, and the grizzly female that feeds on the meadow well below the sheep with her two spunky youngsters knows it too.

On the opposite slope, on a little moist meadow within the alpine firs and Engelman's spruce, feeds a red-coated mule deer buck. Its large antlers are in velvet and the antler tips are swollen and shiny. The buck's neck is thin and elegant, quite different from what it was last fall, or what it will be again in but another two months. He has no facial mask; his face is not much different from that of a doe. He is now at peace with other bucks and intent only on feeding and scanning the surroundings for anything suspicious.

In spring, bucks start to associate in
"bachelor groups" and begin to migrate to
the higher elevations that eventually constitute
their summer range. The mule deer buck of spring
bears little resemblance to the prime buck of the
previous fall. Its sprouting antlers are in velvet,
their tips black and shiny. The buck's neck is
slender and his winter boat is in the process of
shedding, leaving him ragged and unsightly.
After the long harsh winter months, he
has also lost much of his bulk and
appears almost emaciated.

This is a meadow he knows well, just as well as he knows this mountain and this remote part of the valley. Year in and year out, ever since he followed a large buck here as a yearling, he has returned to this valley, this mountain and this meadow. So have other large bucks he got to know. There are no strangers here. He left the winter range little more than a skeleton draped in a shaggy, badly worn winter coat. His antlers had barely begun to sprout then. Yes, he was thin, very thin and lucky to be alive another summer.

Like so many other mule deer bucks in the Rockies, or on the many mountain chains to the west, this buck is out to again prepare his body for the supreme test – the next mating season. His body needs renewal and repair after the long winter's fasts and hardships. During winter his bones grew thin as they dissolved to supplement nutrients in his meager forage. His fat stores remaining after the rut were utilized to supplement his daily energy intake. His fat, along with his liver, had acted as storage sites for precious vitamins that were not available in adequate amounts in the winter feed. He had shed his old winter coat in late spring, and with the beginning of the new plant growth, grew a red summer coat. Simultaneously, he mobilized the last of his body reserves and began growing a set of antlers, long after he had shed the old ones on the winter range, somewhere below and far down the valley.

The buck was choosey about what he ate. He had to be. The summer was not that long, and the nutritional quality of the plants, in particular their protein content, would deteriorate soon. He stripped the leaves from long willow shoots as if he knew that he would have to look long to find a forage richer in phosphates, calcium and protein than these willow leaves. These leaves contained, of course, more then essential nutrients. They also contained

*Summer means the return of lush
vegetation to mule deer country. Now
the animals can selectively feed on highly
nutritious forbs and browse, which they can
rapidly digest and, if necessary, detoxify. Deer
are often attracted to salt and mineral licks to
obtain supplements necessary to their diet.
This doe has uncovered a bison jaw
near a lick and is mouthing it
to pick up nutrients.*

large dosages of acetylsalicylic acid, a toxin we use in aspirin, but the buck's rumen and bacterial flora were most capable of detoxifying various plant poisons, as were his large liver and kidneys.

The buck is a concentrate feeder, a specialist in selecting and digesting highly nutritious, but often toxic, parts of plants. The bighorn sheep, by contrast, concentrates on grasses and sedges. These are toxin-free, but much harder to digest and they require a longer fermentation time in the sheep's complex stomach. To allow a longer time for fermentation of the grass fibers, the sheep has to have a much larger rumen, a longer caecum, a longer gut, but a smaller liver than the mule deer buck.

The deer fed somewhat greedily, as he had just risen from his bed, and his rumen signalled an urgent need for filling. After feeding on the abundant willow leaves he would begin nibbling on the flowering parts of various alpine herbs. He would also go to the mineral lick at the foot of the mountain, following the deep trails that generations of bighorn sheep, mountain goats, moose and elk had worn into the hillside. It was actually no lick as such, it was a cold spring that spewed out a reddish precipitate and smelled a little like rotten eggs. It contained sulfate salts. The buck did not know it, but his rumen flora was capable of incorporating the sulfates into their structural protein as the amino acids cysteine and methionine, both not common in the deer's plant forage. Since the buck would digest the bacteria and other unicellular organisms that grew and flourished in his rumen, he would get the rare amino acids and other organic substances the rumen flora had synthesised. These included many vitamins. Cysteine and methionine are vital amino acids for growing hair,

On hot days, mule deer seek shade and lay down to keep cool. This buck, lying in the cool shadow of a river bank, finds its extended leg an open invitation to a horsefly.

hooves and connective tissue throughout the body.

The buck was soon meandering. He had finished feeding, and so had another buck who emerged from behind a clump of alpine firs. The big buck laid down, and the second buck approached and did the same. However, he was careful to lie down in such a fashion as not to look into the other buck's face. That is a matter of courtesy among deer. One does not look at another's face. One looks away. Consequently, when deer lie down they act as if looking in various directions, as if covering every angle so that a predator's approach could be detected. There is, on closer observation, little evidence for that hypothesis; the simpler explanation is that deer are trying to avoid looking into each other's

Unlike females, mule deer bucks tend to be found more at higher elevations, and more often in the subalpine in summer. The division is not absolute. Rich forage in areas burned by wildfires, wherever such may be, also attracts and holds bucks. Bucks, unlike does, must gamble on rich forage to grow to maximum size. Only by growing large and powerful are they likely to become master bucks, only by storing plenty of fat can they last long enough during the very demanding rutting season.

Consequently, the quality and quantity of forage must be the buck's primary concern in summer. By ascending in elevation the buck can keep pace with the slowly upward-moving sprouting of vegetation. After all, spring and green-up come first to the valley bottom and last to the north sides of upper elevations. By far the best foods are the young, nutrient-rich, virtually toxin-free shoots. For a buck to maximize its intake of such shoots, it needs to follow the wave of sprouting vegetation up the mountain.

When a female mule deer recovers her fawns from their hiding places, she is very attentive for any potential signs of danger. Fawn nursery areas are often located in thick cover near water and suitable forage. Here a doe cleans her fawn's anal area to reduce scent that may attract predators. Even without her fawns as visible evidence, this doe is obviously nursing, as indicated by her large, extended udder.

At this time of year the females, after bearing fawns, look haggard. They need cover for the security of their fawns, but they also need high-quality forage to produce milk. They tend to compromise forage quality and quantity in favor of greater security for their fawns. And that means that the females are more likely to stay in cover in the lowlands than are the bucks. Small creeks rich in low willows, sedge meadows, fire weeds, and grasses growing from flooded scree are favorite places for female mule deer. These creeks carry silty melt-off waters that deposit the highly fertile silt along the water courses. That, in turn, allows rich forage to grow there.

While a buck must maximize its body size to dominate other bucks, the biological requirements of a doe are different. She does not need to maximize the growth of her fawns during pregnancy, she only needs to ensure an *optimum* birth size. Fawns which are too large pass the birth canal with difficulty and suffer higher mortality than do fawns somewhat smaller. Of course, very small fawns, grown during gestation on a poor diet, also suffer a high mortality. Successful fawns are born of an optimum size, not too small and not too large. Of course, a rich milk supply ensures rapid growth to survivable size. However, even here the female need not gamble away security for food. Mule deer fawns spend a long time in hiding. As long as they are in hiding they are relatively safe from predators. A maximum of growth would only make them "followers" a few days earlier, and if anything, make them more vulnerable, not safer. Thus the female can compromise food for safety and still contribute many offspring to the next generation.

The different behavioral adaptations, or survival objectives, of the two sexes

*Mule deer fawns are born in the spring
soon after the does have reached their summer
range. The gangly offspring weigh from six to
seven pounds at birth. They give off very little
scent and remain motionless when bedded. These
traits and their camouflage coat help foil predators
such as coyotes, bears, eagles and bobcats. Fawn
mortality is a natural occurrence and can be high
after severe winters. This fawn died in its
hiding place among some rocks.*

consequently pull does and bucks into different habitats, just as differences in bodily ability between sexes generated differences in their anti-predator strategies.

When the fawns regularly emerge with their mothers at the end of summer, the yearlings also seek out the company of the fawn-leading does. The red summer coat of the deer is now dropping out as the gray winter fur becomes visible between the red hairs. The bucks are in their gray, but still short-haired winter coat, by the first week of September. Even the fawn-leading females begin to look filled out and sleek; they are the last to shed and regrow their winter fur. They are held back in their own restitution by the need to produce milk for the fawns, and, thus, they are about two weeks delayed in the shedding cycle.

Now the bucks begin to show a mask on their faces. Their antlers are fully grown under the fuzzy, furred velvet, and there is little doubt from their rounded body contours that they have grown fairly fat. One can sometimes see large groups of bucks together, though more usually one finds them in small groups or alone. However, a buck alone today may be with others tomorrow and alone again the next day. They roam over a fairly large summer range and return with regularity only to the mineral lick.

I knew such summering bucks as individuals during several summers when I worked in Banff National Park. They were entirely tame and allowed me to follow and observe them. They also paid short visits to our cabin and rested near it sometimes before moving on. Unlike bighorns, they were never pushy, and also unlike bighorns they demonstrated clear instances of insight and willful individuality. I began following one buck with my film camera. When he moved, I moved. When he stopped, I stopped. Suddenly, the buck made the

Having shed its spotted coat, the buck fawn on the top left looks very much like a small doe. Now in the winter coat, the buck is recognizable by the small antler pedicles beginning to grow above its eyes. In summer when food is abundant, deer may occasionally be seen playing, most of which involves running games.

connection. He stopped feeding and looked at me. Then he bounded off about 50 paces and turned around to look at me. The moment I had shouldered the camera and made one step in his direction he turned and was gone in a few bounds. The following day I met the same buck again, and, to my great relief, he allowed me to walk up as if nothing had happened. However, I had also learned my lesson and never again allowed an animal to grow uneasy in my presence. I either stepped away and pretended to do something else then watch it, or I left for the day. As we were able to show many years later in experimental harassment studies, mule deer really panicked if "addressed," that is, singled out for attention.

Bucks that know one another show little sign of aggression or appeasement. Some display to one another, but this is rare. When it happens it is not different from the regular type of dominance displays that are performed at other times of the year. Only at the narrow access to the mineral lick may a large buck displace a smaller one by raising a front leg and striking it. Yearling bucks in their summer coat and velvet antlers may join the older bucks and follow one or another temporarily. They are quite curious about the large bucks and stare at them. Large bucks noticing this avert their eyes and look away.

Subordinate bucks are allowed to look. They are also allowed to approach and sniff the tarsal glands of the large bucks. The yearling bucks do not remain with the older males but move off and may be seen with females and fawns, then again with a young buck, then with a yearling female and then again alone - and so on. There is much moving and mixing in late summer and fall.

The shedding of antler velvet comes to the large bucks very suddenly, in the second

and third weeks of September. In a couple of days it's all over. The velvet splits along the upper tines, revealing bloody, white bone surfaces. The affected buck thrashes his antlers in shrubbery, and soon the velvet hangs loosely down about his eyes and ears. It remains attached to the base of the antlers the longest, giving cause for the buck to work his newly exposed antlers into the shrubs and young trees about him. However, bucks with velvet hanging about their faces may feed and act as if not bothered by these strands of bloody skin.

After polishing antlers, the bucks remain for not much more than a couple of weeks on the summer range. Then they drift to the distant rutting and winter ranges. The areas they formerly used reveal old beds sprinkled with long, red summer hair. The bucks are rather massive now and have bulging bellies. Their necks show a little swelling already, but it's a far cry from the diameters to which their necks will swell when in rut.

The first snowfalls have come and melted away, and during a few nights the frost was so severe as to kill the herbaceous vegetation. The bucks still feed avidly, but now on seed heads, on the last service berries, on poplar leaf hay and on frost-killed and cured, or "ensilaged," vegetation.

To observe a mule deer buck feeding in fall in the foothills of the Rockies is to see one of the more convincing demonstrations that mule deer select easily digested, soft, nutritious plant matter. In fact they turn into "detritus" feeders. Its all due to the natural "silage" that begins to form soon after the first heavy frosts have killed off the herbs and turned the aspen and poplar leaves to their fall colors. The process of natural ensilage formation begins when the frost-killed herbs have dried out. The frosts break open the living cells so that

After the first frosts of late summer or fall, dried,
fermented herbs are a favorite food of mule deer.
This natural ensilage will be eaten throughout
the winter as long as supplies are found.

the poisons that protect the leaves drain out. Then bacteria and fungi attack the dry leaves and break down the plant fiber, converting the dried leaf to fungal filaments and sugars. Mule deer immediately feed on these fermenting plants. Their favorite, soon stripped to the last leaf, is the tall (and in the green state quite toxic) false hellebore, with the toxic cow parsnip ranking a close second.

After the first frosts the Russian thistle is also eagerly sought out for food by mule deer; so are stinging nettles and myriads of herbs such as Siberian aster, baneberry, false solomon's seal, fire weed, and balsamorhiza. A major food source is the dried yellow leaves of balsam poplars. One cannot help but be reminded of potato chips when standing near deer that are loudly crunching one dried balsam leaf after the next.

Leaf hay from poplars is even more popular. This forms on branches that have broken off in summer storms when the leaves were still green. A deer finding such a treasure rarely leaves before the branch is stripped to the last leaf. Moreover, these dried leaves are dug out from below the snow and are part of the deer's menu right through winter into early spring. Deer are not fond of poplar leaves once such become wet and turn dark brown. But crisp yellow leaves they adore! But not the leaves of aspen. Why so, I do not know. Also high on the list of favorite foods are the wilting leaves of red osier dogwood and willows.

The "windfall" of food does not stop here. During wind storms, Douglas firs lose their terminal twigs. It so happens that in trees toxins are more likely deposited in the lower than in the higher branches, while scraggly shoots may be particularly toxic. Terminal twigs from the upper branches should be therefore least toxic. Mule deer may feed heavily on such

*Bucks are attracted to areas of vegetation
such as this one containing dead cow parsnip
(Hercleum) stems, in the foreground. Mule deer
are also attracted to waterways, not only to drink
but to find vegetation near shore, such as the
alpine fireweed, a preferred forb.*

fallen twigs, in addition to the beard lichens that are knocked down with them, as well as the terminal buds of old poplar trees that topple to the ground.

This diet is balanced against some feeding on evergreens, such as oregon grape and prostrate juniper. Deer also search out the sparse sprouting grasses along trails in fall. In Waterton townsite the mule deer excavate green lawns from below the snow blanket, favoring the long, soft strands of the red fescue. Browse constitutes strictly a starvation diet, which they begin to feed on after high snow on the ground makes other foraging uneconomical.

CHAPTER 5

ALLIES & FRIENDS

*In mule deer populations, the big,
large-antlered bucks are usually, but
not always, the dominant males
that breed most of the does.*

*Although a buck's antlers may change from
year to year, it is possible to identify individual older bucks by general antler shape, ripped
ears, rump patch and tail markings, body color
and distinctive facial markings. These photos (top)
showing the same buck were taken two years apart.
The animal is past its prime and regressing. The
two bottom photos show the same buck
from one year to the next. Older bucks'
antlers tend to be more asymmetrical,
and atypical antlers are
not uncommon.*

From mid-October onward, the large bucks arrived one by one on the females' ranges. They were familiar figures to me. I had seen them before, for all the bucks returned with great loyalty to the same area to rut. Their antlers were a little different from the year before, but not always; some bucks of modest size seemed not to change at all from year to year in antler shape. Others changed due to age, for the peak in development is reached by mule deer bucks at about eight years of age. Thereafter, the antlers become more asymmetrical and smaller until the buck returns with only two long, wavy spikes. However, regressed bucks can continue to play an active role as dominant bucks, even those who only have spikes.

I could still recognize these regressed bucks by their distinct faces, rump patches and injuries. And I always had photos from the year before to aid in identification. As with ourselves when aging, so the bodies of the very old bucks changed; they became much more massive and usually had little trouble intimidating big bucks with much larger antlers. It is usually enough for the huge old-timers to approach their prospective rivals in a determined dominance display to affect the young bucks' retreat. None of these younger contenders usually remains behind to test whether the old bucks can back up their threats.

Besides exploring the valley in a casual manner, testing an occasional female they encountered and stuffing themselves on natural ensilage, the bucks met and stayed with other bucks, at least for temporary company. Yearling and two-and-one-half-year-old bucks sought out the big bucks and appeared intrigued by them. So was the occasional female mule deer that suddenly stared at a new arrival, then circled to its rear, ducked and crawled closer to sniff the buck's tarsal glands. The buck acted "cool," as if ignoring it all.

There were three female clans holding big home ranges along the valley. Invisible boundaries segregated the clans, boundaries formed largely by natural features, but arbitrary in other places. They were not sharp boundaries, but, for instance, females from one group would not cross a certain ridge east, and the neighboring group would not cross the same ridge west. One would find the same group of females on a designated area, but not females of any of the other groups. Within these very large areas, measuring one to three miles in diameter, the female clan members usually moved about in small groups, though occasionally they united.

There was no fighting between clans in fall, though there was plenty within each group, directed mainly by adult does at yearling does. Nor was there any obvious leadership, except in the smallest clan, where a very old doe was the center of attention. She was not dominant, nor was she leading a fawn of her own, but others followed her. And if the others did not follow her lead, she patiently stood and glanced back at them until they turned and followed her. She was a source of attention to fawns that grouped about her and followed her. She was very friendly to passing clan members showing the little courtesy crouch which is particularly prevalent in white-tailed deer and is less conspicuous, though present, in mule deer. When we studied this small clan the old female was no longer good at running and showed her extreme age in her gaunt features. Still, she was the center of attention.

The two larger clans remained on location year in and year out, but the smaller one broke up and vanished, leaving a deserted area that was not colonized by mule deer for several years. The clan dissolved with the disappearance of the old female. Where my students and I had followed, watched, filmed and photographed these deer, no more mule deer were to be found for some four years, until the study ended. But a decade later I have again seen mule deer there.

When mid-winter came, the clans deserted their accustomed ranges and moved up into a neighboring valley. The small clan then moved out as a unit and returned in early spring, again as a unit. As a unit, the small clan also aggressively confronted other deer when joining other clans to form the large wintering herd. The clans were thus real, natural units. However, predation did disrupt them severely. The death of the old female is one case in point. The dispersal of clan members under heavy coyote predation is another case in point. Still, when the deer in our study fled areas with intolerable predation, they did so as groups, not as individuals.

Had my colleagues and I been able to mark the females and fawns in our study, we would have been able to discover so much more about the behavior of clan members and the function of the female clans. Based on the study of roe deer and whitetail clans, we suspect that those of mule deer are similarly made up of members united by maternal descent. While it is easy to record in unmarked deer the strife surrounding yearling does in fall, it is not at all easy to determine the ultimate fate of these yearlings. While some does could be easily identified individually, others could not be, and it was thus not possible to follow their fate in an exacting manner.

Nor could the fates of yearling bucks be as easily followed as those of older bucks. Too great are the changes that yearling bucks undergo while growing up, and too great is the influx of yearling strangers and the exodus of familiar yearlings. However, from two and a half years of age onward, one can confidently recognize the bucks individually, year after year.

During the rut, female clans are each claimed by a large "master buck" who keeps out other large bucks but tolerates the presence of some smaller bucks. The other large bucks are usually drifters, and a few are non-breeders as shall be discussed later. All this is readily visible as long as a persistent pack of coyotes does not disrupt the deer. For if one does, as was the norm in the last years of one of my studies, the deer were as if wiped from the landscape. All one saw were traveling bucks seeking out the dispersed, hidden females. Also, the bucks carried more wounds than previously. Eventually, the deer did leave the area, except for a few individuals, and detailed observations became scarce and difficult to achieve. When the clan structure was evident, however, it was also evident that the same master bucks and smaller satellite bucks were present on the same clan range.

When the bucks arrive to socialize with one another in late October, they engage in common, often long-lasting rituals: sparring matches. To the uninitiated, a sparring match looks like fighting. It is not. It's a sporting game and a means of forming bonds of "friendship" between bucks. Bucks on "sparring terms" are friends, and the smaller sparring partner makes use of his friendship with the bigger partner to insult and displace other, bigger bucks – with his bigger friend's help. This is a hint of the complex social factors involved in mule deer society.

Sparring in mule deer is of an "asymmetrical" type and very different from the sparring matches carried out by elk, for instance. In the elk, sparring partners *both* approach in dominance display as *social equals*, at least for the purpose of sparring. (Later, after the sparring

Sparring is a common behavior that serves
to form "friendship" bonds between bucks.
Young bucks continue to spar with one another
throughout the rutting season.

phase and when actual competition for breeding females begins, the truly aggressive encounters of male elk take on a different purpose. They do settle rank and order then.) In the *sparring* matches of elk, though, there are neither perceived winners nor losers, neither dominants nor subordinates. Consequently, theirs is a symmetrical engagement of "equals."

By contrast, mule and white-tailed deer sparring matches are asymmetrical because the sparring partners retain their individual distinctions in dominance rank. The larger buck continues to use the signals of dominance, and the smaller uses signals associated with subordinate status. Also, elk sparring partners engage simultaneously; in the sparring matches of mule and white-tailed deer, though, it is the smaller who initiates antler contact. This is true in spite of the fact that the larger buck may have solicited the sparring match, followed the smaller partner and shown appeasement behavior towards him. To an uninitiated observer, this latter behavior can be most confusing. However, large bucks do solicit sparring matches from specific smaller bucks and may work patiently to convince that buck to initiate sparring.

A muddling factor is that very small bucks, yearlings usually, appear among older bucks and show obvious interest in them. These yearlings may stand and stare at them, but the big boys look away. The youngsters will then circle to the rear of the large bucks to smell their tarsal glands, which are particularly odorous – even to human noses – in old bucks. The old bucks not only urinate regularly on their tarsal brushes and rub them together, but they also do not lick off the urine, as do females and small bucks. Subordinate bucks in the company of dominant ones fail to contribute to the scent of their own tarsal glands because they squat and urinate like females. Their urine thus falls straight to the ground, bypassing the tarsal glands.

*All mule deer urinate by squatting, as
exhibited by the doe in the upper photo on
page 110. While rutting, however, older bucks
urinate on their tarsal brushes and rub their
hind legs, and thus the brushes, together
(bottom photo). Yearling bucks do
not exhibit this behavior.*

That is the normal way for bucks to urinate outside the rutting season or in the presence of larger bucks. It is also the appropriate way for the smaller of two sparring partners to urinate, whereas the larger usually passes its urine over its tarsal brushes.

Let us assume a small buck has snuck up and tested a big buck's tarsal glands and remains standing, looking over the big buck who, in appropriate mule deer etiquette, has his head down and is feeding. One now notices that the larger deer slowly shifts his position so that his antlers are tilted towards the small buck. Then he pauses, head lowered, antlers pointing toward the smaller buck, and waits. This is soliciting. More likely than not, the small buck will now accept by lowering his antlers and engaging the larger buck.

But matters are not always that simple. Sometimes a large buck follows and solicits repeatedly but is snubbed by the smaller male. The larger may then crouch while feeding. In mule deer, both feeding and crouching are, in their sign language, submissive behaviors. Performed by a larger buck to a smaller they are appeasement gestures. The soliciting large buck will carefully "feed" himself into the path of the smaller buck, blocking his way, then slowly present his antlers in an attitude signifying an invitation to spar.

Once the smaller engages, the initial sparring is cautious and akin to a friendly bout of human arm wrestling in that the bucks twist their necks with their antlers "hooked" about one another. The disengagement is done by the smaller, who suddenly jumps backwards and turns his body and eyes away from the large buck, who also turns his head away from the smaller buck. This "eye aversion" is part of the ritual. After a distinct pause in rigid eye aversion, the smaller is likely to turn and signal re-engagement. The larger complies and the

*Sparring does not involve two bucks making
headlong rushes at each other. Instead, the two
deer engage antlers relatively softly, then twist
and pull to offset the other deer's balance.*

bucks again begin to wrestle and push mildly. This rhythm of disengagements by the smaller, followed by re-engagement by the smaller, may go on for up to an hour. However, as the bucks spar, engagements become less hesitant, the eye aversion becomes less rigid, and it may happen that the larger starts the re-engagement instead of the smaller. The sparring bout terminates with the smaller buck turning to feed. The larger then follows the smaller and feeds and rests with him.

Sparring matches among these two bucks, now on "sparring terms," may now be initiated by the larger, instead of the smaller buck. For instance, the larger may suddenly move from feeding and engage antlers on his resting, smaller partner. A larger buck may repeatedly try to engage the smaller one, who patiently refuses every time without running away. The larger, after each failed sparring attempt, averts his eyes for several seconds before following the smaller to try again or to resume feeding.

The most unusual scene, at least for ruminants, is to see the smaller sparring partner suddenly move in full dominance display at a much larger, strange buck who has joined the group. The large stranger is likely to be hesitant in responding with a counter display that threatens the little imposter, for the little buck's big sparring partner often will suddenly hurry after his smaller friend and rush the large stranger, putting him to flight. The smaller one, rubbing it in, may then rush after the departing stranger in full dominance display. In one case, however, I witnessed the tables turn quickly. The stranger moved over a hill out of sight of the large sparring partner and quickly ran off the small buck, who had arrogantly followed him over the hill.

*Sparring engagements between mule deer are not
violent but are more analogous to friendly tests of
strength such as human arm wrestling.*

The sparring partnerships last several days before the bucks split up, prior to the rut, but I have repeatedly seen smaller, former sparring partners with master bucks during the rut. I have witnessed these master bucks briefly chase off their former sparring partners when they approached too close to an estrus doe. However, these are mildly aggressive encounters when compared to the hostility the master bucks show towards strangers.

I have also seen such satellite bucks copulate with does within the master buck's realm. The best hypothesis to account for all of this has to do with the sparring bonds several small bucks may form with a potential master buck. He and his smaller satellites control a clan range. The satellites are tolerated, more or less, and take on bucks of equal size that venture onto the clan range. This leaves the larger male free to court and breed, and be diverted from this occupation only when a very large challenger shows up. Even so, at the height of the rut the master buck cannot pay attention to all females coming into heat, which allows the satellite males to do some breeding.

Sparring among bucks older than two years is concentrated during the days before the females come into heat, which in the Rockies begins about November 15. Another wave of sparring, a much smaller one, can be observed at the end of the rut, which comes about December 10. Sparring is executed in the same fashion during both periods, but clearly with less vigor during the second one.

Sparring exhibits little oddities: Large bucks sparring with small ones may compensate the mismatch in antlers by only extending one antler for engagement. In white-tailed bucks I studied on the Texas gulf coast, small bucks might lie on their belly and circle a

larger buck, then – from this belly-to-ground position – lick the face of the dominant buck and, while licking, rise, roll their antlers forward into those of the larger deer and commence sparring. Otherwise, the sparring by whitetails is similar to that of mule deer. A bit of this face licking, a primitive white-tailed deer behavior, is occasionally seen in small mule deer bucks, who begin licking their own lips before engaging the larger partner.

One can observe literally hundreds of sparring matches before seeing one real fight, for serious altercations are very rare between mule deer. In fact, even a tenacious observer might go a whole rutting season without seeing a serious battle, despite being in daily contact with mule deer. Having an opportunity to witness such a conflict is a relatively rare privilege. A fight among mule deer bucks is a spectacle worth watching.

CHAPTER 6

RANK & POWER

*When horning, bucks may sometimes spend
considerable time stripping and eating the bark
they fray from the trees with their antlers.*

*Mature bucks vigorously "horn" to locate
one another during the rut. After horning
a tree or bush, a buck will stand
quietly and listen for a reply.*

The social behavior of mule and white-tailed deer is similar, with some notable differences. These differences are especially pronounced in courtship behavior, which forms a one-way ethological barrier to hybridization, as we shall discuss later, but there are also, within each species, some differences in the behavior of bucks to one another.

The basic signal elements of whitetail and mule deer, however, are clearly the same. Bucks of both species urinate on the tarsal glands while rubbing these together (urine-rub), a behavior shared with moose and caribou. In the urination posture there is a difference: The mule deer buck squats while urinating, exactly like the female, whereas the whitetail buck only crouches. In both species, subordinate bucks may look directly at dominant ones at close distances while the dominant bucks avert their eyes. Both species practice conspicuous eye aversion to punctuate pauses during sparring matches. Both have asymmetrical sparring, even though the initiations differ somewhat, as described earlier. Both species render a "rut snort" during dominance displays and exhibit only minor differences in postures while executing this display. Both "horn" shrubs and trees, the mule deer very often and in drawn-out sessions, the white-tailed deer much less and for shorter periods. Fighting is relatively rare in both species, compared to sparring. Both have "courtesy crouches," although that gesture in the white-tailed deer is much more expressive, as is its submissive behavior. An observer watching the respective bucks in action would have no difficulties concluding that mule and white-tailed deer are closely related.

When a large mule deer buck spots a large untested rival, it commences to approach

*All-out dominance fights between bucks of
equal size are rarely seen. Horning precedes
antler contact in these contests, and the buck
with the uphill position will generally have the
advantage of gravity in the ensuing battle.
(Photo sequence continued on page 124.)*

the adversary in dominance display. He literally shows off! Large strangers tend to reciprocate. The bucks approach one another at an angle. Their movements are stiff; the tail is raised and the hairs are erect all over the body. The bucks' heads are slightly averted from one another and the antlers tilted away from the opponent. The ears are laid back. The tarsal glands are flared widely, and the preorbital glands are open. As the deer come closer together, their movements slow down further and they lower their bodies closer and closer to the ground. When a few paces apart, they begin circling one another slowly and stiffly.

At this point a fight can still be averted if one buck suddenly grunts and blows sharply through his nose (rut-snort) and the other bounds away in response. The "blower," now dominant, may rush after the loser, putting him first to flight and then escorting him away for a mile or more. The rut-snort of a large buck invariably makes smaller bucks flinch and jump. However, if the rut-snort is ignored by the displaying opponent, a fight is inevitable.

When an all-out fight begins, the bucks rush at one another with such suddenness and speed, and fight with such quick and complex motions, that the eyes and mind of a person observing the action have difficulty following it. The engagement is close to the ground; crouching is now seen as a protective behavior shielding the bucks' underparts from a sudden attack. Also, the deers' bent hindlegs allow instant anchoring during the clash. The rivals push with great ferocity, but then reverse and pull. An opponent suddenly pulled off the ground may be thrown over the "puller's" back and land on the ground with a crash, ending the fight. The bucks may also spin about with locked antlers, or one may attempt to gore the other in the side. Among their other functions, then, antlers obviously serve as weapons as well as tools for

catching and neutralizing the opponent's attacks.

Combatants may rest a moment during fighting when one buck pushes the other's antlers into the soft ground and holds them there. Both will then pant heavily. Shortly, however, the melee will resume, each buck trying to throw his opponent off balance. The combatant that eventually loses his footing will usually be the loser in the fight. Usually, that buck will manage to suddenly disengage and bound off, the winner pursuing him and goring at his haunches. During the pursuit the victor will hit the ground hard with his front-legs and utter a series of sharp, deep, rough "pursuit" grunts. This send-off behavior is observed in many deer species.

I have never found a locked set of mule deer antlers or a buck killed in combat. Still, wounding is common during combat and may be severe but not necessarily debilitating. An examination of tanned hides indicates that mature mule deer bucks sustain some 30-50 wounds per year. Some of these wounds are large and deep, but most are short tears and punctures and cannot be readily seen, even when one sees blood on the buck's body. Wounds are well hidden by the animal's hair. I once tracked a large buck who was dripping blood, and even after an hour of looking at him from a distance of a few feet I could not see his wound. This buck's antlers were coated with frozen blood. I took off back-tracking, hoping to find his victim, but a heavy snowfall set in, obliterating the track.

Once a buck is defeated in combat it is invariably escorted by the master buck beyond the borders of the female clan's range. This may not be easy, for a defeated rival may try to circle back repeatedly. However, each attempt is cut off by the dominant buck, sending

*Two bucks approach one another, ears lowered
in dominance display. The buck on the left, which
has an abnormal jaw, soon submits to the more-
dominant male, however, and moves away from
it to begin feeding. The brief encounter concluded, the
dominant buck also begins to feed.*

the rival scurrying. The winner follows in dominance display; he rut-snorts periodically, urine-rubs and horns trees and shrubs during the pursuit. When the defeated rival has given up and heads off in a straight line, the winner may watch him disappear and then, confident that the subordinate has left the area, return to his home range.

The subordinate may meander on, his hair and tail pressed close to his body, a sign of insecurity. After a while the defeated buck may begin horning the branches of a bush, hesitantly at first. Then horning quickens and may accelerate to a frenzy while the buck's tail rises and his penis becomes erect. The buck may stop his frenzied horning and suddenly rut-snort while his hair becomes erect all over his body. This behavior possibly represents a buck "psyching" himself out of a defeat. I have seen such bucks flinch, apparently in fear, when, upon their first hesitant horning, there was a loud *CLACK!* of their own antlers on wood. They would pause and then hesitantly begin horning again, as if reasserting their aggressiveness. After all, it takes a "brave" buck to make a racket with his antlers!

Horning in mule deer is a little like bugling in elk. Big mule deer bucks use horning as a form of sound-location to find one another. Follow a large, roaming buck and it soon becomes evident. Periodically, the big buck will stop and horn a shrub loudly, then pause and listen. He will do this repeatedly during his wandering, until suddenly there is a reply in kind - another buck "answering" by horning. That sound is pinpointed by the first buck. He then horns again. His horning is answered. Up goes the hair on his body, down go his ears and the buck is off in the direction of the horning rival. The next reply may be a lot closer. That will mean a serious challenge. The bucks meet, initially, as if by accident, and in dominance display

circle one another until one leaves and is escorted away by the other.

However, bucks may also indulge in horning without the explicit purpose of addressing other deer by sound. They may use their short brow tines to deeply gouge thick branches of trees. They may deposit secretions from their frontal organs during this rub. They may fray the soft bark from branches and then nibble, strip and eat such bark. They may also rub their face and neck on the bark or leave a moist spot on it where they have rubbed their nose against it. Whatever additional function this behavior serves is uncertain, but horning appears to stimulate a buck's bravery as subsequently he is likely to urine-rub copiously.

In one important respect mule deer bucks differ from white-tailed bucks: They form no scrapes. In all the years that I observed rutting mule deer I saw one buck scrape three times with a front leg after horning the overhanging branch of a spruce tree. Here was a last echo from ancestral genes. The scraping ritual so carefully examined in recent years by biologists studying white-tailed deer is normally not found in mule deer. It appears to be compensated for by extensive horning. That, however, has no apparent function in attracting mule deer females, except, maybe, indirectly. After horning, bucks urinate copiously on their tarsal glands, and the resulting scent is at least a curiosity to female mule deer. A big, rutting mule deer buck is terribly smelly, and we know from studies of the moose that male urine is a powerful attractant for the female, and it is at least suspected to be so in white-tailed deer.

In small-bodied species of deer, urine scent is disassociated from the rutting male's body, while in large cervids such as moose, elk or caribou it is distributed over the male's body. This distribution is usually accomplished by urine-soaking the mud in a wallow, and then

distributing the mud over the body and neck mane, a behavior common to elk and most Old World deer. In addition to wallowing, the moose also splashes mud onto its bell, or neck "wattle." In caribou the tarsal scent is spread over the bull's face when he rubs his rostrum all along his hindlegs.

In its behavior the white-tailed deer appears intermediate between small and large-bodied deer; it urine-rubs over the scrape, and thus impregnates itself as well as the ground. However, a large white-tailed buck is simply never as smelly as a large mule deer buck. Nor are his legs as matted with urine as are those of a large mule deer buck. The larger the buck, the more it urinates on the tarsal brushes, spraying thereby the hindlegs with urine from well above the tarsi downward. The mule deer, clearly, has opted to side with large species and carries his urine scent on his body. This behavior may be related to the mule deer's relative lack of geographic fidelity as compared to white-tailed deer, and the large areas he traverses.

Urine-marking, horning and dominance displays are part and parcel of a large buck's behavior towards fairly large rivals when defending a female in heat. Small bucks are not so honored. Small bucks are likely to be rushed by the master buck and gored, unless they are able to escape. Such chases, however, do not greatly discourage small bucks, for they soon return.

Bucks sort out their dominance order by the first week of November, well before the females come into heat. The master bucks are in place on the clan ranges by then, repelling other bucks. Conversely, most of the subordinate bucks, large ones included, are drifters without fixed whereabouts. They move about casually, checking out the hidden, favorite areas

*While in the rut, mule deer bucks reduce
but do not eliminate feeding. Because of the
large amount of energy they expire during
the reproductive season, bucks lose a great
deal of their body mass despite their
continued feeding activity.*

of does, while avoiding the dominant bucks.

At this time, yearling bucks will still spar, but the large bucks no longer do. All bucks, the most dominant included, still feed, but their bellies are noticeably smaller and drawn up higher. Their necks are swelled. Reproduction is about to commence.

However, not all bucks will participate in the rut. This came as a surprising discovery. While the majority of bucks will be in the rut state, a few bucks will not. These few on my study area were the very largest of bucks. (One in particular carried exceptionally massive, long-tined antlers. It is still the largest mule deer buck I have ever seen.) At first I thought these quiet monsters were anomalies, cowards destined to become reproductive failures. It was certainly intriguing to see these large bucks feed, rest and ruminate while most other bucks were in full swing with the activities associated with rutting. These non-rutting bucks, however, ignored bucks with esterous does, avoided the master bucks and were generally left alone by other bucks, possibly because of their massive proportions. I followed these large fellows and noticed that they were certainly watching what was going on about them. They even urine-rubbed, acting much as one would expect of a large buck. What was wrong with them?

As it turned out there was nothing wrong with them. However, it took some time before I discovered what they were up to. Among the bucks I got to know early was a large, dark buck who was horribly defeated by a massive, old, regressed master buck in the first year of my study. I named the dark one O-buck. He had rutted normally enough until he held his ground against the master-buck's challenge, and promptly got into a fight. The fight was all

*Two bucks challenge one another, loudly and
violently horning nearby conifers. They then close
and circle, crouching low to the ground, but, when
the buck on the right right lowers its antlers,
preparing to charge, the other buck bolts away.*

over in seconds as O-buck was jerked free of the ground and flung upward; he fled instantly –
and quit rutting.

The following year and the year thereafter O-buck also failed to rut. Then a harsh
winter removed the large bucks. O-buck, with his fat stores largely intact, survived. Now there
was no one to challenge him and O-buck became the master buck of the valley. For three years
running he bred heavily and repeatedly. This "coward," far from being a reproductive failure,
was probably the most successful breeder of all the bucks I observed.

It appears that male mule deer may thus follow one of two strategies: either to try to
become a normal master buck, with all the costs that this entails, or to "opt-out" of the rut
altogether, waiting out periods of severe reproductive competition. This allows these non-
competitive bucks to retain their fat stores and thus survive harsh winters that kill active
master bucks who use up their fat stores during the rut. The bucks that opt out naturally grow
huge antlers because antlers are initially grown in spring from body reserves, and the non-
participants should have the largest body reserves. They are also expected to grow to
exceptionally large size because they have relatively less body tissue to replace following
injuries during the rut and suffer less weight loss in the ensuing winter. The efficiency of this
strategy is enhanced if there is a population decline following a severe winter. Granted that the
"opter-out" may breed the same number of does a successful master buck had bred in earlier
seasons. The "opter-out," in fact, breeds a relatively larger fraction of the now decreased female
population.

When female mule deer start coming into estrus,
bucks will roam widely in search of receptive
does and mating opportunities.

The "opting out" strategy, clearly, must be confined to locations where, for whatever reasons, the mule deer population fluctuates greatly over the years. Then the master buck strategy wins when the population is high, and the "opting out" strategy wins after a population decline. ❦

CHAPTER 7

MATING FURY, CLEVER TRICKS & WINTER SURVIVAL

Frost and cold don't disturb mule deer.
Hardy animals, they are adapted to living in
cold climates as far north as the Yukon Territory.

*Any fallen tree, in this case a lodgepole
pine, is welcome winter food.*

The rutting season of mule deer begins in late fall and is usually in full swing by the middle of November. Snow normally covers the ground along the Rockies by this time; the first blizzards have swept the land but powerful, warm "chinook" storms have repeatedly cleared the snow from the foothills and prairies. Each storm finds the deer retreating to dense fir or pine forests to find shelter. Each storm also shakes off a new shower of douglas fir twigs or topples old poplar trees, both welcome forage for mule deer.

The deer may also wait out the storms in the rolling hills, where, as long as deer stay about one third down from the top of the wind-swept hill, they are virtually unaffected by winds. While blizzards howled overhead, I have spent many hours in the hills with the deer. Rarely did they venture out into the gales and blowing snow. When they did, they quickly galloped through it to the safety of another pocket of calm air where they nonchalantly commenced feeding. I had a terrible time crossing the same wind-swept areas, despite my excellent clothing. Canadian blizzards seem to cut through everything you wear, blind you with blowing snow, numb your face and stop your breath. I certainly did not purposely go out to see how mule deer made out in blizzards, but I got caught outside in terrible weather a number of times and learned quickly to adopt the ways of the deer. They knew exactly where to find shelter and food during the gales. These winter storms, I also observed, did not disrupt the rut. The bucks continued to test does.

During courtship, even in a raging snow storm, a mule deer buck tests does by first trying to obtain a sample of urine from the chosen female. Once that sample is available, he will perform a crucial test to determine whether or not the doe is close to estrus and decide whether

When courting does a mule deer buck approaches them in a low stretch posture and attempts to solicit urine from them. This female (top right photo) has conceded to urinate for a courting buck. The male will test the sample to determine if the doe is in estrus and receptive to copulation. Bucks test does' urine by performing a lip curl, or flemen, which causes the entrance to the Jacobson's organ, located on the buck's upper palate, to open.

to follow the doe or to try his luck elsewhere. While male ruminants, including the white-tailed deer, tend to have one method of obtaining a sample of a female's urine, the mule deer buck has two ways. In fact, the mule deer is the only ungulate I know of that has two entirely different methods of courting.

Most commonly a mule deer buck solicits urine by closely approaching the female in a "low-stretched" posture. He licks his nose and utters soft calls reminiscent of the distress call of a fawn. In effect, he plays "baby." His sharply intonated facial expression becomes a signal, part of the courtship ritual: Should the female look back, she would see the buck's face as a much accentuated "fawn face" and low to the ground. This parasitizing of maternal emotion would appear to be a fine way to hold a female's attention and prevent her from running off.

The courting buck may then touch the female with his muzzle and then instantly avert his eyes. He also interrupts whatever he may be doing and averts his eyes if the female glances up at him. Again and again the buck "addresses" the female, squeaks, even touches her, then looks away. In response the female feeds and avoids the buck by making a little half circle around him. She does not run away; she too appears to be at least a little interested. With seemingly infinite patience the buck will continue to court the female – until she finally squats and urinates. While young bucks cannot wait and often stick their noses into the urine stream, usually disturbing the female, old bucks wait until the female is finished. Then they step forward and perform the "lip-curl," or "flemen," a chemical test to determine the doe's stage of estrus.

*Big bucks tend to stay in the vicinity of doe
groups just prior to and throughout the rut. Any
buck appearing on a female clan range prior to the
rut will have its hocks inspected by the does.
Licking of the estrous doe's swollen vulva
by the buck prepares her for copulation.*

In the buck's palate, right on the midline within the pad confronting the lower incisors, rests a small organ called the Jacobson's organ. It is a little pouch lined with ciliated cells which have a direct nerve connection to the brain. During the lip-curl this pouch opens and admits the odor of the female urine. We suspect this organ to be the chemical sensor that alerts the buck to the female's reproductive state, which, in turn, is indicated by the chemical makeup of her urine.

There is a second way for the mule deer buck to get the female's urine. Since a lot of bucks "request" urine from a female, and since she can get rid of these pesky bucks only by urinating to them, she has to ration her urine lest she run dry. Consequently, it is not in her interest to urinate promptly and copiously to every passing buck; after all, the soliciting buck might leave and try another female. At the same time, it is very much in the buck's interest to make the female urinate so that he can get on to test as many other females as possible. Therefore, when a female holds out on urinating, the buck may grow impatient and do something about it. This begins with the buck throwing what could be described as a temper tantrum. First, and quite suddenly, his body becomes rather stiff while his upper lip begins to quiver and a high-pitched tone emanates from his throat. Even though the females nearby may still feed, all suddenly become uneasy and watch the buck intensely. They had better! Suddenly the buck will hurl himself – antlers lowered – at the courted female and roar at her. While she departs instantly, the buck gallops after her in hot pursuit, slams the ground with his front-legs and bellows with every jump. (Tanned hides reveal that females do carry antler scars and this is probably when they get them.) This merry chase covers a couple of hundred yards. Then the

Precopulatory mounts are very common in mule deer.
When copulation does occur, the buck bounds
upward and his hind legs may leave the ground.

buck stops in a low-stretch posture and the female also stops – and urinates. Fright, evidently, is another behavioral stratagem used to make the female urinate if less aggressive courtship fails.

The sexual interests of many small bucks may drive females to seek some respite from their attentions by staying close to the master buck. That leaves the small bucks circling the master buck and his females. This also makes the master buck appear to be standing within a harem. However, a harem this is not, for the master buck does not herd the females into a harem. He exercises control strictly over the one female he is interested in, namely the female that is in estrus or is about to enter estrus. His behavior is thus quite unlike that of a bull elk, which does defend and herd a harem.

While the master buck focuses on the female about to enter heat, he nevertheless chases off any young buck that dares court a female within his sight. However, the master buck chases off some bucks with more determination than others, despite the fact that there are usually one or more small bucks close to him and the doe he is guarding.

In mule deer, breeding is a much drawn-out affair compared to white-tailed deer breeding, both before and after copulation. Mule deer copulation is preceded by a slow progression of behaviors beginning with the buck's licking of the female's vulva, followed by him putting his neck on her croup, progressing to him touching her with his chest, and finally followed by the first pre-copulatory mount. The first mount is followed by a series of mounts, usually more then five, though I once counted as many as 43. These pre-copulatory mounts are fairly long, often lasting more than 15 seconds. During the mount the buck may or may

A doe in heat, her estrus usually lasting about
two days, will be closely attended by a dominant
buck, even during blizzard-like conditions.

not put his weight on the doe. When the copulation comes, though, it is a powerful thrust that lifts the buck off the ground. About one-third of the females bleed thereafter, and all begin a series of powerful belly contractions. This reaction by the does is another difference between mule and white-tailed deer copulatory behavior.

Not all does are bred as described. There may be complications. The very first doe in heat may be with a master buck, who, highly excited, appears to have forgotten how to breed. At such times the doe may court the buck intensely, for several hours! She dashes from him, circles him while frolicking, butts him, rubs her head over his haunches and croup, attempts to mount him, and may even strike him with a foreleg along his side. Meanwhile the buck stands there terribly stiff, letting it all happen, or follows the female, low-stretching to her and averting his eyes. Such female courtship is also common towards the end of the rutting season when the big breeding bucks appear to be totally exhausted.

When copulation begins, the pair becomes isolated. The doe is bred repeatedly during her estrus period, which lasts about a day. However, the pair is not safe from small bucks that crisscross the clan range in search of a breeding opportunity. The defending buck pays close attention to them, and with good reason: These small bucks have a clever strategy for separating the master buck from the doe in order to try to breed her. Suddenly, one of the youngsters stotts in high bounds at the pair, blowing sharply with each jump. This is the most extreme of alarm behaviors. As a matter of course the doe bolts, and the young bucks bolt after her. The breeding buck then runs after them, trying to keep up as best he can.

I do not know how far these chases may go or how often the small bucks succeed in

losing the master buck, or if the doe permits them to breed. All such chases that I saw terminate were, of necessity, short ones in which the master buck quickly reestablished control. I have certainly seen estrous does alone with satellite bucks and being bred by them, but then the master buck may have been occupied elsewhere. In such cases, as might be the case when the master buck intercepts a large, straying buck, the satellites are right there with the estrous doe, trying their luck. This is courting suicide if the big buck returns and the youngster is preoccupied. However, mule deer bucks display incredible agility when bounding out of the reach of another buck's antlers.

During the three-week period when females come into heat, the bucks noticeably lose physical condition, particularly the large bucks that do most of the breeding and fighting. Their antlers show broken points, their coats are streaked with combat damage, their sides seem caved in as the muscle contours on their bodies become visible, and they appear dazed. Large bucks quit rutting very suddenly, from one day to the next. They then lie about in thickets, totally exhausted. They once again squat like females when urinating and ignore all females and bucks, at least for a few days. Sparring may again be observed among the bucks, especially among the young, subordinate males. The rut has run its course – the next challenge is to survive the winter.

In this post-rut period the mule deer's behavioral repertoire is once again directed to security. The big bucks initially disperse, to recover in hiding. Then, about three to four weeks after the rut, they emerge, shed their antlers and join the wintering female herds, probably to take advantage of the superior security within the "selfish herd." (The term "selfish herd"

*An older buck bleeds from the point of attachment
of his recently shed antler. This wound,
however, will heal quickly.*

points to the fact that each individual joins with others for a selfish reason: It is more secure from predation within the herd than outside of it). Here they mingle in quite inconspicuously and even urinate exactly like females. Picking out bucks in these mixed herds is difficult and possible only if one can identify the buck's facial mask – should he look up. The buck, having shed his symbols of "maleness," appears to use females as a camouflage. Bucks exhausted by the rut cannot be expected to be enduring runners, and carnivores would quickly recognize the link between conspicuousness and a weakened animal. However, if the carnivore cannot readily distinguish between buck and doe, and if does greatly outnumber large bucks, it becomes very difficult for the carnivores to recognize the rut-weakened bucks within the herd. (Young bucks, which come through the rut in better condition than old bucks, shed their antlers later. While they may be conspicuous, they are also capable of running with more speed and endurance than exhausted old bucks. Consequently, they are less endangered by keeping antlers on their head.)

A number of relatives of the mule deer – as well as in pronghorn bucks, where the behavior was first described by Dr. Peter T. Bromley – use this "camouflage" strategy. The large males shed their antlers or horns and join female herds to become inconspicuous. By contrast, in species where rut-exhausted males retain their horns or antlers, they segregate from females and move into superior escape terrain. Regardless of the survival value the camouflage strategy imparts to exhausted bucks in post-rut buck-doe herds, though, there is still nothing more dangerous to an individual in the selfish herd than to be less capable of running than the majority of its members, and thus find itself at the tail end of the escaping herd – where the hungry predators are.

*During and after the period of antler shedding,
bucks join groups of does and form what
are known as "selfish" herds.*

Mule deer often, but not always, assemble in large overwintering herds that exploit the wind-swept areas of the foothills and prairies. In some areas it is white-tailed deer that form the large herds on the prairies while the mule deer remain behind in the hills, segregated in small wintering bands. Such segregation takes place soon after the rutting season in the Cyprus Hills, a large tract of tall, forested hills surrounded by prairie in southeast Alberta. With the descent of heavy snow, white-tailed deer flood out of the hills to band into large herds on the open, wind-swept prairie. Differences in anti-predator strategies explain this segregation. The hills have large tracts of low rose and snowberry bushes that are nearly impossible to traverse except along trails well worn into the shrub blankets by livestock and wildlife. Windblown snow soon covers up all the trails, precluding any speedy running by white-tailed deer, but not speedy stotting by mule deer.

Mule deer also winter in sagebrush flats in the prairies, foothills and semi-deserts. Such lowland winter ranges may be reached only after lengthy migrations. Wherever mule deer live in tall mountains, seasonal migrations between winter ranges in the valleys and summer ranges at higher elevations are normal. That such migrations are food-related is demonstrated dramatically during unseasonably warm winters in British Columbia when mule deer remain year-round on the summer ranges. Where mule deer are too scarce to form large selfish herds they may seek security in steep coulees, in sharply cut badlands, or in pockets of dense shrubs or forests that grow in the wind shadows of hills. They emerge in small groups at dusk to feed, and they withdraw at dawn.

Mule deer, as concentrate feeders with the ability to detoxify plant poisons, can feed

After the rutting season, about the time
they begin to shed their antlers, bucks once
again become gregarious. Deep fluffy snow is
not an enemy but a friend of deer. It preserves the
quality of forage and provides a good bed for resting.
When they do bed down to rest, mule deer position
themselves so they do not look directly
into each other's face.

avidly on plants containing various oils and waxes, such as sagebrush or juniper. However, the deer require supplements from other plants because they rapidly loose condition when on a pure sagebrush diet. As a relatively small-bodied ruminant with a low metabolic demand in winter, mule deer have time to precisely search for and select an adequate diet. Large-bodied ruminants cannot be as selective. They need to ingest a much larger amount of food in the same time. Thus mule deer can continue to search for small amounts of green, low-toxic tissue as are found in overwintering sedges, fescues or blue grasses, or the dried berries of the snowberry bush, or the dried poplar leaves and cured herbs protected from deterioration by a layer of dry snow.

The selfish herd protects the bucks well until the winter is over. Then they join other bucks, forming male associations, or "boys clubs," while the females segregate by clans and drift back to their early winter ranges. By now all the deer show the ravages of winter, but particularly the surviving bucks. They are little more then skeletons draped with skin. Their ribs can be counted by even the most casual observer. Even such survivors as O-buck, who skipped the rut, are gaunt, despite going into winter with large loads of fat on their bodies and about their internal organs, metabolic salts in their bones and vitamins in their liver and fat. The hair on the deers' bodies is weather-beaten and ragged. The bucks' antlers are not yet growing, but soon will be, and soon, too, the bucks will begin the drift upward to the distant summer ranges.

Now, with the snow nearly melted off, one can see some curious examples of deer adaptability. The storms of winter have piled high masses of hard-packed snow beyond the

In winter, mule deer will reach for whatever browse is available, including twigs on overhead branches. Serviceberry (top right photo) is not only favored for its fruit but also for its twigs and buds. A nip at a Douglas fir (below) sends snow cascading down on a hungry mule deer.

crests of hills, along the crests of ridges and on the lips of coulees. These snowdrifts, which invariably occur in the same places each year, are fertile with silt and support rich plant communities in summer, for the snowdrifts supply not only moisture during the slow melt-off but also contain extra nutrients that are mixed into the snow when chinooks scour the exposed, dry earth.

Many of these large snow drifts form within aspen-covered bluffs. The aspen tree pushes out catkins early in spring, and while mule deer show little enthusiasm for aspen leaves, green or cured, they avidly search out the budding catkins. They reach these catkins by climbing on top of the tall snow drifts. Thus the hard-packed snow provides deer with localized access to the crowns of trees and their highly nutritious shoots. In late summer or fall, after the snow drifts have melted, I point to the crowns of aspen some ten or more feet above my head and explain to a visiting colleague that deer browse there. A perplexed facial expression is inevitable as he scans the distance between the ground and the tree tops. 🐾

CHAPTER 8

THE MULE DEER'S END?

For all its current abundance, the mule deer, so different, so uniquely American, so young and promising, is nevertheless a species marked for extinction.

For all its current abundance, the mule deer, so different, so uniquely American, so young and promising, is nevertheless a species marked for extinction. That may be its fate in the long run. Either the white-tailed deer or man may cause that extinction. Without either, the mule deer could continue unimpeded for as long as habitats exist and the sun rises. It got along well enough with white-tailed deer as long as we were not around, but conditions changed with our arrival.

The mule deer has already lost much of its former range. It is now found in Manitoba only as an exceptional stray where it once was common, and it has suffered sharp declines in the prairie provinces of Canada where white-tailed deer replaced it within a few decades of appearing on mule deer range. Mule deer show signs of dwindling wherever they meet whitetails, even in the mule deer's stronghold in Wyoming, and now apparently also in Texas. The white-tailed deer, the genetic wellspring that gave rise to the mule deer, may determine the fate of the mule deer in more ways than one.

No, the two species do not compete. Both are "anti-competitors," specialized as ecological opportunists, and both have shown themselves to be inept competitors when meeting Eurasian deer species in New Zealand, Europe and North America. Our deer, ecologically, need not displace one another over a struggle for material resources. Mule and white-tailed deer segregate ecologically by occupying different types of escape terrain and cover, which reduces competition for material resources a priori. They also differ vastly in escape strategies and tactics as reflected in the features of the respective terrains they occupy. To predict where mule or white-tailed deer will be found, then, one needs to understand their

Adult female mule deer bond in
clan units (above) and are aggressive
toward young females, especially strange
young females that attempt to join the clan.
Two bucks (bottom photo) rear and flail
at one another with their sharp hooves
in a dispute over access to choice,
sprouting tufts of grass.

anti-predator strategies; what they feed on or where they feed is of secondary concern. Both species may move between feeding and bedding areas at dusk and dawn, but where the two species bed, an element of their respective anti-predator strategies, will differ greatly.

Nor is the white-tailed deer so aggressive as to displace mule deer. If anything, the opposite is likely as mule deer normally dominate white-tailed deer. Moreover, white-tailed deer show every sign of being quite uneasy in the presence of mule deer. For instance, white-tailed deer females crawl on their bellies in a submissive posture when passing mule deer does; white-tailed bucks coming in sight of mule deer stop and scan the mule deer, then turn and walk away. Outside the rutting season, both species may be in close proximity, such as a whitetail buck joining, temporarily, mule deer bucks, or whitetails and mule deer feeding in a scattered wintering herd. There is no convincing evidence or observations that white-tailed deer displace mule deer from their ranges through overt aggression.

Diseases and parasites? There may be a little more to this suggestion. The white-tailed deer, as an ancient species, carries a host of co-adapted parasites that are highly dangerous to other deer species. Foremost among these is the meningeal or brain worm (*Paraelaphostrongylus tenius*) of the whitetail. It is lethal if transmitted to other cervids. Other parasites that cause grief to other deer species are the whitetail's ticks (*Dermacentor albipictus*) and the giant liver fluke (*Fascioloides magna*). The former is a debilitating plague of moose and, of recent, also of caribou, while the liver fluke, transported to Europe with introduced white-tailed deer, is most damaging to roe deer. Is it possible that white-tailed deer transmit something lethal to mule deer? The only candidate that would fit this hypothesis is the

Mutual grooming about the face, ears and neck is common between yearling siblings and between young-of-the-year and their mothers.

meningeal worm, which mule deer do not tolerate as well as whitetails do. However, the meningeal worm terminates its range in western Manitoba, yet white-tailed deer have supplanted mule deer in Saskatchewan and Alberta to the west. One can never exclude the possibility that some unknown lethal organism is transferred from whitetails to mule deer, but even if such an organism exists, it can only compete in the destruction of mule deer along with a much more potent factor. That factor is one-way hybridization.

Let me explain briefly a hypothesis that arose out of our work and the work of colleagues concerned with deer hybridization (in particular, William D. Wishart, who started looking at the problem in Alberta, and Susan Lingle, who did the experimental work described below). To the best of our current knowledge, white-tailed deer and mule deer are effectively reproductively segregated by two ethological barriers and one physiological one, the infertility of hybrid males.

One ethological barrier is the incompatibility of courtship between mule deer bucks and white-tailed does. The second is the dominance of mule deer bucks over white-tailed bucks when defending estrous does. One of these ethological barriers is destroyed by human interference – hunting, which removes large mule deer bucks more efficiently than it does the secretive, often nocturnal white-tailed bucks. This, in turn, leads to large white-tailed bucks displacing minor mule deer bucks and then breeding mule deer does. The result of that union are hybrids that survive well, as long as they are with their mule deer mothers. Once alone, they are nonviable because their anti-predator strategies and tactics are a non-functioning mixture of incommensurable strategies and tactics of their parents. Consequently, each hybrid

*Mule deer do not hesitate to enter
water. On the Pacific Coast, blacktails
are renowned swimmers.*

is a loss of mule deer reproduction. And where mule and white-tailed deer meet, the decline of mule deer is almost inevitable because of reduced mule deer reproduction due to hybridization. While one would wish this hypothesis to be much better supported by available data than it currently is, it is nevertheless one we have to take very seriously.

Breeding between mule deer bucks and white-tailed deer does is incompatible, because upon the approach of bucks from either species the female white-tailed deer is prone to run. This is normally not done by the mule deer doe, and if it is done, then the mule deer doe runs in relatively small circles. Moreover, should a mule deer buck attempt to pursue a white-tailed doe on the run, he is hopelessly outclassed by the speed of the white-tailed deer. Yet there are exceptions to this, for very rarely a white-tailed doe with a hybrid fawn is encountered.

A mule deer doe usually allows the approach of a courting buck. She would most likely be unable to outrun a white-tailed buck. One notable exception to this would be in the steep-sloped badlands. Here a mule deer doe, intent on escaping a buck, can ascend straight up the hills. That's no problem to a stotting mule deer, but it would be a problem to a galloping white-tailed buck. I have never seen a white-tailed deer ascend steep, long hills on a full run. It also appears that hybrids between mule and white-tailed deer do not occur in the badlands where both species live side by side. In a heavily hunted area in Alberta, for example, where whitetails and mule deer have survived in sand hill country, an area of low, but steep hills, no hybrids are encountered. Hybrids appear to be concentrated where both species live in forests.

All observations to date indicate that mule deer dominate white-tailed deer of equal

*In many areas of its range the mule deer
is ecologically segregated from whitetails,
occupying higher elevations and utilizing
different types of vegetative cover.*

or smaller size. My colleagues and I have seen white-tailed bucks dominating mule deer bucks only when the mule deer buck was noticeably smaller than the white-tailed bucks. As I noted earlier, white-tailed bucks that saw the rutting mule deer I studied usually turned and left and only exceptionally showed any interest in mule deer does.

I have seen large bucks of both species fight conspecifics. The mule deer differs by having the more massive neck (for twisting) and by his preponderance to pull an opponent off its feet. Also hard to describe objectively is the pronounced "ferocity" of the attacking mule deer buck. I also think the fact is significant that mule deer and blacktails attack predators much more readily than do whitetails; it suggests a much less timid disposition in the former. More detailed observations and experiments would be welcome here.

That mule deer bucks are easy to hunt, and that heavily hunted populations soon include little more than yearling bucks and have a lopsided sex ratio in favor of does, is a common observation. Conversely, white-tailed bucks are more difficult to hunt and appear to be less susceptible to hunting mortality. This is the least certain point, for studies on differential susceptibility of mule and white-tailed deer to human predation are scarce in wildlife management literature. I know of only two such studies. Both are in agreement with above expectations.

Susan Lingle, in a detailed study of the locomotion of mule deer, white-tailed deer and hybrids, experimentally investigated with the theory that hybrids wind up with non-functional sets of anti-predator strategies and tactics. Her experiments included observations of confrontations expected to elicit strategic, as opposed to tactical, responses. (A strategic

response is comprised of tactical components. Thus, for example, mule deer attacking coyotes is a strategic response; stotting is a tactical component that executes this strategy.) Both sets of experiments showed that the mule deer x whitetail hybrids were behaviorally debilitated or deficient. Her study also established that these strategies and tactics were innate, or under close genetic control.

In response to an encroachment by a man with a dog, for example, whitetails would flee. The mule deers' response to the same situation would be to approach and mob or attack the dog. The hybrids, however, would stand and neither flee nor mob. When chased through a series of obstacles, white-tailed deer skirted the barriers, mule deer stotted across the route, but the hybrids hesitated and picked their way through the obstructions. These are examples of hybrid behavior indicating deficient strategic responses.

As examples of the hybrids' tactical incompetence, in response to disturbances they would bound in a slow and clumsy manner. When galloping they showed inefficiencies during landing and were somewhat slower than either parent species. In concurrence with these experimental observations of the maladaptive behaviors of hybrids, lone hybrids in the wild appear to be unusually tame. Hybrids, in other words, are hardly functional deer.

What can be done to save the mule deer?

There are a number of responses possible, all hard decisions and none very palatable. Exterminating white-tailed deer on mule deer ranges or manipulating habitat on a massive scale to deprive white-tailed deer of security are neither practical nor feasible solutions. Likewise, promulgating hunting regulations that would affect a decrease in the

number of large white-tailed bucks and allow a relatively large number of large mule deer bucks is hardly a cheerful prospect for hunters. It would mean foregoing virtually all hunting of large mule deer bucks where mule and white-tailed deer overlap. Clearly, gaining public support for such a management policy would require a herculean effort. In the meantime, however, we can assuredly expect mule deer will continue to lose ground to the whitetail.